Month-by-Month
Trait-Based
Writing Instruction

**Ready-to-Use Lessons and Strategies for Weaving
Morning Messages, Read-Alouds, Mentor Texts, and More
Into Your Daily Writing Program**

Maria P. Walther
&
Katherine A. Phillips

SCHOLASTIC

New York · Toronto · London · Auckland · Sydney
Mexico City · New Delhi · Hong Kong · Buenos Aires

To my kindred spirits, primary grade teachers!
M. P. W.

To Mom and Dad, there is no mini-lesson or morning message that can help me find
the words to express how grateful I am to you for all of your love and support.
K. A. P.

Acquiring Editor: Virginia Dooley
Development and Production Editor: Gloria Pipkin
Cover design: Brian LaRossa
Interior design: LDL Designs
Copy Editor: Carol Ghiglieri
Cover photo © AAGAMIA/Getty Images
Interior photos courtesy of the authors and Lenny Walther

ISBN-13: 978-0-545-06693-8
ISBN-10: 0-545-06693-X
Copyright © 2009 by Maria P. Walther and Katherine A. Phillips
All rights reserved. Published by Scholastic Inc.

7 8 9 10   40   19 18 17

Contents

Morning Message Menu

	Ideas	Organization	Word Choice	Voice	Conventions	Grammar and Usage	Words for Writers
September	Think Small! (37)	Let's Sort (39)	Show, Don't Tell* (38) Word Exchange: **fun** (37)	Show, Don't Tell* (38)	What Do You Notice? (34) Looking at Letters (35) Spaces Between Words (36) Where Do the Periods Go? (36) Mixed-Up Names (39)	Nouns All Around (38)	September Word Chart (35) The Letter Stealer—Consonants (39)
October	Discovering Details (57)	Using Riddles to Teach the Concept of a Sentence* (55)	Word Exchange: **scared** (59) Thesaurus Thursday (60)	Whose Voice Do You Hear? (60)	Using Riddles to Teach the Concept of a Sentence* (55) What Kind of Sentence, Telling or Asking? (57)	What Is This Sentence Missing? **verbs** (60)	October Word Chart (54) The Letter Stealer—Short Vowels (59)
November/ December	The Mystery Character (75) Looking for Ideas? Tell Us How You Feel Today (77)	Comparing Characters (74) Settings and Senses* (76)	Settings and Senses* (76) Word Exchange: **went, cold** (78)	Reread Your Piece Aloud With Voice (77)	Creative Conventions (78)	Sorting Nouns, Verbs, and Adjectives (76)	November Word Chart (74) December Word Chart (74) The Letter Stealer—Long Vowel/Silent e (77)
January	Real-World Writing (94)	Let's Write a List (95) A Friendly Letter* (96)	Word Exchange: **friendly letter closings** (96)	Who Will Receive This Letter? (98)	Commas in a Series (97) A Friendly Letter* (96)	Singular and Plural Nouns (96) Past- and Present-Tense Verbs (97)	January Word Chart (94) The Letter Stealer—Word Endings (95)
February	Roses Are Red Poems* (114) Interviewing Interesting Individuals (116)	Chronological Order (115)	Roses Are Red Poems* (114) Word Exchange: **like** (115)	First- or Third-Person Voice* (116)	Capitalizing Proper Nouns* (115) First- or Third-Person Voice* (116)	Capitalizing Proper Nouns* (115)	February Word Chart (114) The Letter Stealer—Digraphs (115)
March	Piggyback Songs (130) The Leprechauns Were Here! (129) Poets Write About Things They Love* (131)		All About Alliteration (130) Rhyme Time (131) Word Exchange: **bright** (129)	Poets Write About Things They Love* (131)	The Conventions of Poetry (128)	Vivid Verbs (132) Amazing Adjectives (132)	March Word Chart (128) The Letter Stealer—Blends (129)
April/May	Nonfiction! (145) Narrowing Nonfiction Topics (145) Nonfiction Acrostic Poems (147)	Categorizing Nonfiction (146) The Features of Nonfiction* (147) Let's Label* (148)	Word Exchange: **hot, looked** (146)	Writer of the Day (148) A Fond Farewell (150)	The Features of Nonfiction* (147) Let's Label* (148)	Contraction Match (148)	April Word Chart (144) May Word Chart (144)

* Lesson addresses more than one component of balanced writing instruction.

Mini-Lesson Menu

	Ideas	Organization	Word Choice	Sentence Fluency	Voice	Conventions	Grammar and Usage	Words for Writers
September Genre Exploration: Telling Our Story—Personal Narrative (49)	Let Your Ideas Flow! (41) Writing Is Hard Work! (42) Writers Get Ideas From Their Lives (43) Creating an Idea Notebook* (44)	Creating an Idea Notebook* (44)	Word Swap (48)	Tap Your Toes and Stamp Your Feet—Listen to the Author's Beat (47)	We All Have Our Own Unique Voice (46) Showing Feelings in Your Writing (45)	Why Are Conventions Important to My Reader? (48)	People, Places, Things, and Animals = Nouns (46)	Chop It Up! Introducing Developmental Spelling (44)
October Genre Exploration: Crafting a Story— The Basics (70)	Looking for Ideas? Reach for a Wordless Picture Book (63) The Details of Your Day (67)	The Building Blocks of Organization (66)	Adding Action to Your Story* (66) Let's Collect Words (68)	Searching for Sentence Fluency (70)	The Who and Why of Writing (69) Details Add Voice to Your Illustrations (69)	Question Marks (70)	Introducing Verbs (64) Sentence Sleuths—Nouns and Verbs (65) Adding Action to Your Story* (66)	Working With Word Families—A Useful Spelling Strategy (64)
November/ December Genre Exploration: Crafting a Story—The Elements (91)	Questioning the Character (81) Settings and Senses* (83) Identifying Events in Mentor Texts* (87)	What Kind of Lead Do I Need? (80) The Big Ending (89) Identifying Events in Mentor Texts* (87)	Introducing Adjectives—An Alphabet of Adjectives* (82) Settings and Senses* (83) Using Similes to Describe a Character (81)	Can You Combine These Sentences? (84)	Add Voice to Your Illustrations With Speech Bubbles (88) Different Versions = Different Voices (87)	Exclamation Marks (90)	Introducing Adjectives—An Alphabet of Adjectives* (82) Creating an Adjective Chart Using a Thesaurus* (85)	Chunk It! A Strategy for Spelling Multisyllabic Words (84) Creating an Adjective Chart Using a Thesaurus* (85)
January Genre Exploration: Penning a Letter—From Postcards to Persuasion (111)	Let's Write a List (100) Jot It Down!* (100) A Letter of Advice to a Nursery Rhyme Character (108) Write a Book Blurb (103)	To Squish or Not to Squish—Write a Persuasive Letter (109) Jot It Down!* (100) Mapping Ideas (101) Write a Recipe (110) The ABCs of Organization (104)	Yikes! I Have And-Itis!* (105)	Let's Build a Sentence (105) Yikes! I Have And-Itis!* (105)	Write a Friendly Letter* (106)	Write a Friendly Letter* (106)	Playing With Prepositions (107)	
February Genre Exploration: Writing a Biography—Future Famous Americans (124)	Learning Lessons From the Past (118)	Categorizing Facts About Famous People (121) Time-Order Organization (120)	Transition Words and Phrases* (121)	Transition Words and Phrases* (121)		What Are My Initials? (123) Abbreviations (122)	Noticing Proper Nouns (119) Common and Proper Nouns (119)	Using the Word Wall to Spell High-Frequency Words (123)
March Genre Exploration: Composing Poetry—Playing With Words (141)	Poets Write About Things They Love* (133) Poets Write About Things They Know—Exploring School and Animal Poems (134)	Poets Use Shape—Concrete Poems (138)	Poets Use Sound Patterns—Alliteration (135) Poets Use Sound Words—Onomatopoeia (135)	Poets Use Rhythm—Repeated Lines (137) Poets Use Rhyme (138)	Poets Write About Things They Love* (133)	Poets Use Creative Conventions (140)	Poets Use Vivid Verbs (139)	Poets Use Sensory Images (139)
April/May Genre Exploration: Delving Into Nonfiction—From Research to Writing (160)	The Wide World of Nonfiction (152) Nonfiction Poetry* (156) Grabbing Your Reader's Attention* (158)	The Features of Nonfiction Texts (153) Expository Text Structures (155) Topic Sentences* (158)	Synonym Bingo (159) Grabbing Your Reader's Attention* (158)	Nonfiction Poetry* (156) Topic Sentences* (158)	Let's Pretend (157)	Conventions Review—A Punctuation Bee (160)	Grammar Review Games (159)	

* Lesson addresses more than one component of balanced writing instruction.

Acknowledgments

This book is brimming with ideas because we are fortunate to be surrounded by people who nudge and support us as we spend countless hours trying to do what's best for kids. Thanks to . . .

- Our Tuesday Night Team, especially Sue Lambert, Mary Blessing, Sarah Cooley, Kellie Friedheim, Roberta Bree, and Mary Ann Frantzen, who also enjoy reinventing the wheel!

- Sally Walker, Suzanne Zettle, and Paula Jensen for taking time to read our manuscript—your comments and suggestions spurred our thinking.

- The Indian Prairie District 204 Writing Committee past and present, including Kathy Klees, Mary Dolan, Nicole Everix, Liz Webb, Allison Landstrom, and Jan Newport for shaping our vision of quality writing instruction.

- Our first-graders at Gwendolyn Brooks Elementary School in Aurora, Illinois, whose dazzling words and shining faces are our inspiration.

- Gloria Pipkin, editor and friend—the process of writing a book is more joyful when you're cheering us on.

- Our designer, Lauren Leon, who magically blended together our words, work samples, and art.

- Virginia Dooley, whose vision guides us as we create practical professional resources, and Susan Kolwicz, for her marketing magic and willingness to lend a helping hand. We're proud to be part of the Scholastic family.

- Our families and friends, who understand that, for us, spending extra time at school together is fun!

Look for the following icons to help you quickly locate and identify the different types of morning messages and mini-lessons found in this book.

Ideas

Organization

Word Choice

Sentence Fluency

Voice

Conventions

Grammar and Usage

Words for Writers

Genre Awareness

Let's Spend a School Year Together!

We are thrilled that you've decided to join us on this yearlong journey into the world of writing instruction for young authors. Before we jump into the lessons and ideas, we will begin with a bit of background. We realize that you're busy, so let's get started!

A Trait-Based, Balanced Approach to Writing Instruction

We know you have heard and read a lot about balanced reading instruction. However, not as much has been written about balanced writing instruction. As children take their first steps on the path to understanding the craft of writing, they benefit from well-rounded writing instruction. Balanced writing instruction comprises the following elements: words for writers, writing-strategy instruction (commonly known as the traits of good writing), grammar study, and genre awareness. As a primary teacher you might be saying, "Yes, I agree! That's what my young writers need! The big question is, How do I fit it all into a busy teaching day?"

In an effort to answer this question, we've created a framework to demonstrate how the components of balanced writing instruction fit together in a year of teaching. We offer this month-by-month plan as a springboard to get you and your young writers started. Before we embark on this journey together, there are a few suggestions we would like you to keep in mind. First and foremost, you are a professional. For that reason, you are the best person to make instructional decisions to meet the needs of the children you teach. No one else knows your students and your teaching context as well as you do. In addition to having a distinctive teaching context, you also possess a unique teaching personality. Adjust the ideas in this book so that they work for you. View each mini-lesson through your knowledgeable teaching lens. Furthermore, it is important to note that what we offer here is not a rigid step-by-step plan for teaching writing. Instead, we view it as a stroll through a garden of ideas. Along the way, a lesson or two might catch your eye. As a result, you and your students may choose to veer off the main path to delve into a genre exploration, discover more about a specific writing trait, or notice how various authors use a particular convention. Let your students' interests lead the way. That's what teaching writing is all about! Finally, remember that the more you can integrate a writing component into other areas of your curriculum, the easier it will be to find time to fit writing into a busy teaching day.

A Preview of Month-by-Month Trait-Based Writing Instruction

We acknowledge that the learners in our classes differ from those in your classroom. While we have spent our careers in first-grade classrooms, you may be using this book as you teach kindergarten or second grade. Knowing this fact, we open each chapter with an enticing multilevel menu of morning message ideas. A number of the message ideas appear month after month, as a gentle reminder to routinely revisit these writing skills and concepts. Review and practice are vitally important for the diverse learners in our classrooms. While a few students may pick up an idea after one lesson, others benefit from multiple teacher-guided rehearsals before the skill or concept becomes a part of their own writing repertoire.

The morning messages are followed by a selection of writing workshop mini-lessons, along with one genre exploration. We invite you to choose from these menus as you would when visiting your favorite restaurant. Select the lessons that meet the needs of the budding writers in your classroom and that fulfill the standards and objectives of your school, district, or state. If you run out of time in September to teach all of your favorite lessons, remember you have the whole year ahead. We wrote this book to help relieve some of the stress that surrounds planning and carrying out effective writing instruction, so please do not add stress to your teaching life by trying to squeeze in every single lesson. We certainly can't fit them all into one busy month! In addition, we are firm believers in adapting and modifying the ideas of others. As our dear colleague Larry Hatch was known to say, "You ladies are always reinventing the wheel." We encourage you to either use our ideas as they are written or reinvent them to suit your students' needs. After all, our job is to teach young *writers,* not to teach a *writing program.*

Chapter 1

Balanced Writing Instruction

Teaching Writing Is Challenging

When it comes to writing instruction, we know one thing to be true: Teaching writing is challenging! It is challenging because our youngest writers possess a wide range of skill levels, from those who can barely hold a pencil to others who amaze us with their innate ability to write with verve and voice. It is challenging because some students need individualized scaffolding and support to transfer their brilliant thoughts into words. It is challenging because teaching mini-lessons and creating opportunities for meaningful practice takes precious instructional minutes. And finally, it is challenging because we continually struggle to answer questions such as these: *What are developmentally appropriate expectations for my writers? How will I organize and manage my writing workshop time? When will I find moments to confer with each child? Why is there always such a long line of kids at my side?*

As a result of its complexity, writing instruction tends to be the first thing to go when lesson plans overflow or other curricular expectations get in the way. Yet, with all of its demands, teaching writing is one of the most rewarding parts of our day. It is a joy to watch children as they experiment and gain understanding of the complex craft of writing. Without a doubt, the thoughts of a child expressed in written words are incomparable. If only we could all be as candid in our written expression as a 7-year-old!

Hi. My name is Alyssa. My teacher is Dr. Walther for one grade. She likes food and drinks. She is a beauty queen.

Alyssa writes about her teacher!

To assist you in overcoming the difficulties of teaching writing, we've developed this sensible, month-by-month writing guide. We'll start with an overview of the components of a balanced writing approach as outlined in the figure to the right, and then continue with some specific examples of how the components, when blended together carefully, will support budding writers and ease our writing instruction woes. So, where do we begin? Let's get started by identifying the content, or the "what," of writing instruction.

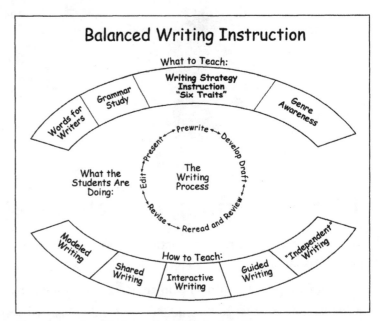

The elements of balanced writing instruction

WHAT TO TEACH

Fortunately, there are many fine resources available to support us in the teaching of writing. Over the past two decades we've learned from the informed voices of writing experts such as Lucy Calkins, Ruth Culham, Donald Graves, Ralph Fletcher, Regie Routman, Vicki Spandel, Katie Wood Ray, and many others. Our writing instruction has been shaped by their knowledge and expertise. Unfortunately, for many of us it is difficult to find time to read their brilliant books and translate their ideas into classroom practice for our youngest writers. We're excited to have the opportunity to do that for you. When you combine our teaching careers, we have spent more than 30 years refining and improving our writing instruction. Even after this book is completed, we will continue to read, question, reflect, and revise our teaching. For this reason, we do not view ourselves as experts but as two teachers who do our best to help students learn about and enjoy writing. With that said, we will share with you what our research-guided experience tells us that primary students need in order to become successful, independent writers. To begin, they simply need words.

Words for Writers

What do we mean by *Words for Writers*? To clarify, Words for Writers is not an in-depth phonics or spelling program; rather, it is a means by which we help our students apply their growing knowledge of phonics to their written work. Our goal for young writers is that they become confident in their ability to developmentally spell words for writing. Developmental spelling is when "Students make their best attempts [at spelling] based on what they know about words—the rules, patterns, visual configurations, and origins of language" (Routman, 2005, p. 162). At the same time, we teach them how to use the print resources in the room to conventionally spell high-frequency and other common words, such as color words, number words, and so on. Without this type of instruction, we would spend valuable writing time helping children spell words when they have the ability to figure them out on their own. Students need permission and encouragement to use developmental spelling because it enables them to write what they know without worry.

Encourage students to use developmental spelling.

Obviously, students who are also engaged in a systematic word study program will be at an advantage when attempting to spell developmentally in their writing. If students become confident spellers, they will build a sense of agency and independence. What do we mean by agency? Peter Johnston, author of *Choice Words* (2004), refers to agency as students' awareness that they can figure things out on their own. To build spelling agency in young learners, we are constantly modeling strategies children can use to figure out how to write a word. In their book *About the Authors* (2004), Katie Wood Ray and Lisa B. Cleaveland offer their young writers some sensible tips to figure out how to spell words. We've adapted their guidelines to match our expectations.

> ### Why Is the Use of Developmental Spelling Beneficial for My Students?
>
> ✦ Encourages writers to experiment with writing longer, more colorful words
>
> ✦ Increases students' writing fluency
>
> ✦ Enhances children's ability to decode words
>
> ✦ Results in increased accuracy as they transition to conventional spelling
>
> (Clarke, 1988; Routman, 2005; Spandel, 2004)

- Picture what the word looks like. Close your eyes. If you've seen it before, do you remember any of the letters in that word?
- Think about what the word sounds like when you say it. Chop up the word, and then write down the letters that stand for the sounds you hear.
- Decide if the word is long or short. Do you need a few letters or a lot of letters?
- Use the spelling patterns we've learned to help you write and spell words.
- Check the word wall. Is it a word we've studied and practiced? If so, spell it conventionally.
- Ask yourself, "Is the word somewhere in our classroom where I can find it?"

We've taught long enough to know that even when you've modeled, shared tips, and celebrated the spelling approximations of your young writers, you will still have those children who refuse to write if they can't spell words conventionally. We offer the suggestions on page 13 for learners of this type.

Each of the chapters that follow features lessons for nudging primary grade students toward conventional spelling. This is part of our job as writing teachers, but it is certainly not the only aspect of writing instruction to include in a balanced writing program. Along with the development of word knowledge, we want to help children to acquire a language for thinking about and evaluating their writing. This is where the traits fit in.

How to Help Persistent Perfectionists—Students Who Only Want to Spell Words Conventionally

✦ Encourage students to take a chance and use the sounds they know to spell words.

✦ Include developmental spelling in your own modeling.

✦ Celebrate young writers' approximations as they share their written work.

✦ Model the fact that making mistakes is part of learning. As Peter Johnston (2004, p. 39) argues, "If children are not making errors, they are not putting themselves in learning situations."

✦ Utilize the print resources developed with your students, such as charts and word banks, to help you spell words as you model your own writing.

✦ Provide writers with handy, easy-to-access resources such as personal dictionaries or word banks.

✦ Confirm students' spelling successes by attending to their partially correct attempts to spell. For example, if a child starts to spell the word *museum* with /mu/, comment, "I see you know how to spell the beginning of that word" (Johnston, 2004, p. 13).

✦ Be patient; this process may take a while. Don't give up! With your support, children will eventually realize that they can write more fluently once they stop worrying about spelling every word correctly.

Writing Strategy Instruction: Where Do the Traits Fit in a Balanced Writing Approach?

The "trait lady" herself, Ruth Culham (2006), defines the role of the traits this way:

> *The six traits represent a language that empowers students and teachers to communicate about the qualities of writing—ideas, organization, voice, word choice, sentence fluency, conventions, and presentation (a feature of writing often added as the "+1" trait). We use the terms consistently, teacher to teacher, year to year, to build understanding of what good writing looks like and to help students generate texts that exceed our wildest expectations* (p. 53).

The traits are *not* a writing curriculum (Culham, 2006) but a fundamental ingredient in quality writing instruction. Wise teachers of writing have known this for years. We regard the traits the same way we view the reading comprehension strategies. Both are sets of common language that offer literacy learners a shared vocabulary to help them examine and learn how proficient readers and writers act and what they do. But reading strategies are not the only thing learners need to know. Undoubtedly, if we taught readers the comprehension strategies without teaching them about phonics, vocabulary, and fluency, balanced reading instruction would be incomplete. Similarly, if we only taught the traits of good writing, students would be missing out on other vital components of balanced writing instruction. When we examine the traits through this lens, we see how critical they are to students. The traits are an indispensable part of balanced writing instruction because they do all of the following:

- Offer a guideline for writing assessment to help students understand how to critique and improve their written work
- Provide teachers and students of all grade levels with a common language to use when discussing and evaluating written work
- Lend themselves to lessons and activities that enhance the writing curriculum
- Supply students with the tools they need to make their writing clear, expressive, and interesting
- Reveal the mystery of writing by breaking down the complex process into manageable elements (Culham, 2006)

Fortunately, trait-based writing instruction is accessible for teachers and engaging for students, and there are a number of fine resources brimming with additional trait mini-lessons:

Inside the Writing Traits Classroom: K–2 Lessons on DVD (Culham, 2008)
Using Picture Books to Teach Writing With the Traits K–2 (Culham & Coutu, 2008)
Wee Can Write: Using 6 + 1 Trait Writing Strategies With Renowned Children's Literature
　　(McMahon & Warrick, 2005)

But, as we noted earlier, the traits alone do not make a writing curriculum. Another crucial component is meaningful grammar instruction. It may be easier to forego authentic grammar instruction or teach it using a prescribed program; however, teaching grammar in the context of writing has a greater impact on the way a student writes and how his or her pieces are read. It is yet another tool that children need in order to convey their ideas in a meaningful way.

Grammar Study

In their review of research on teaching grammar, Michael Smith and Jeff Wilhelm (2006) share some valuable information to guide our thinking in terms of grammar instruction.

- Grammar lessons should occur in the context of written or spoken language.
- Grammar instruction should make sense to students.
- Grammar instruction should be viewed as a way to improve students' writing.

With the above guidelines firmly planted in our minds, we have designed morning messages and mini-lessons that will help young students develop an understanding that grammar will help them as writers. We acknowledge that the trait of conventions typically includes grammar, usage, and mechanics. For the purpose of this book, we are going to focus on grammar and usage during grammar study mini-lessons and on mechanics during conventions mini-lessons.

Genre Awareness

Why do writers write? Writers write for different audiences and purposes. The audience and purpose drive the type of text the author composes. Successful young learners understand how to read and compose different genres. The focus of the genre awareness component of balanced writing instruction is to introduce students to appealing examples of an array of genres found in the world of children's literature and the real world with offerings such as letters, lists, notes, and so on. In each chapter we present a *genre exploration*, which is a one- to two-week venture to guide your students through the creation of a specific type of text from prewriting to presentation. Each exploration is designed to help writers acquire a basic understanding of a specific genre. To assist you in planning, the genre explorations include a helpful chart that defines the genre in kid-friendly language and then offers the following information:

- Characteristics of the genre
- Books to use as mentor texts
- Suggestions on how to differentiate and fine-tune students' understanding of the genre from kindergarten through second grade
- Examples of student work

You will find genre explorations about personal narrative, real and make-believe stories, real-world genres, biography, poetry and song, and nonfiction. Our goal for this component is to use mentor texts and teacher modeling to show students the wide variety of genres that exist and then to give children time to experiment and practice through focused writing experiences.

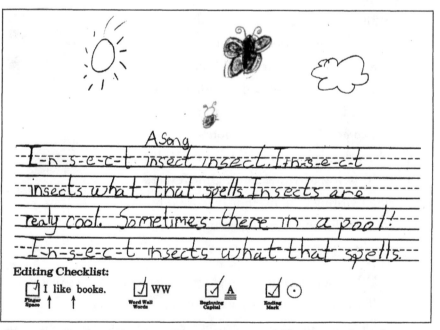

Gianna's song about insects written to the tune of "Camptown Races"

HOW TO TEACH

To review, we've outlined a framework for balanced writing instruction consisting of words for writing, writing strategy instruction, grammar study, and genre awareness. Together, these components comprise the "what" of teaching writing. When we continue to examine effective writing instruction, we also consider "how" we teach writing. And when it comes to teaching writing, we find that along with pencils, paper, and a lot of patience, there is one thing we can't live without—children's literature.

Children's Literature Is at the Heart of Balanced Writing Instruction

We couldn't teach writing without a stack of enticing books. Reading aloud to students and discussing books from a writer's perspective help build students' repertoires of writing possibilities. As you'll soon discover, we have a growing collection of picture books that are ideal mentor texts. Many of the mini-lessons we've included are based on a specific title. We know you also have your own treasured tales, those you enjoy sharing year after year. Select the books you are passionate about to guide your writers. Adjust the lessons to match the literature and the needs of your learners. Trust your expertise and creative abilities to make appropriate book selections for your students. With so much rich literature from which to choose, we are confident this will be an enjoyable part of creating and teaching writing mini-lessons.

In *Library Mouse*, Sam encourages children to become authors.

Why do we use so many books? If you have had the pleasure of hearing an author speak, chances are they've talked about two places from which they get ideas—from their experiences and from the books they read. In fact, award-winning author Avi's fifth secret to good writing is "Read, read, read. Reading is the key to good writing. The more you read, the better the writer you can be. You can NEVER read too much" (www.avi-writer.com). Other experts in the field of writing echo his thoughts. Reading aloud rich children's literature during writing instruction provides these advantages:

- Offers opportunities to highlight specific techniques that writers employ
- Illustrates the endless possibilities open to writers
- Demonstrates that writers choose from a variety of language options
- Provides language patterns and structures for students to borrow

- Shows how different authors approach the same topic in various ways
- Inspires writers to try new things

(Fletcher & Portalupi, 2001; Galda & Cullinan, 2003; Spandel, 2004)

We want our students to understand the vital connection between reading and writing, and we can think of no better way than to read aloud and converse about books from a writer's point of view. Vicki Spandel, author of *Creating Young Writers* (2008), reminds us that "Reading aloud IS teaching writing, even if no writing activity follows the reading" (p. 231). The best writers read widely. Through extensive experiences with books, young writers will come to understand that writing is a conversation with the reader. In the words of the renowned writing expert Donald Graves, ". . . the provision of literature is not a passive event for children. At every turn the teacher seeks to have children live the literature. The most important living occurs at the point at which children *make* literature themselves through writing" (1983, p. 75). With books at the heart of your writing instruction, children are sure to discover the joys of the written word and understand that literature is alive with the voice of the writer. Along with the many books cited in the mini-lessons, you will find a chart in each chapter entitled Read-Alouds for Writers that showcases additional titles to share with your students. How, then, do we incorporate quality literature into balanced writing instruction? We partner the picture books with research-based instruction.

A time-tested teaching model is the gradual release of responsibility approach (Harvey & Goudvis, 2000; Miller, 2002), also referred to as the optimal learning model (Routman, 2005), which progresses from teacher modeling through shared, guided, and small-group literacy work to sustained independent reading and writing. When we gradually release responsibility during our writing instruction, we provide students with the explicit teaching and continuous support needed to learn and apply new writing skills and strategies. As we nudge our writers along on the road toward independence, we carefully plan our instruction to scaffold their learning. Applying the gradual release of responsibility approach to our writing instruction simply makes sense.

Books are the heart of our writing instruction.

As you become familiar with the mini-lessons in this book, you will find that we offer specific suggestions for teacher modeling and thinking aloud. Whether children are just beginning to understand how to label a picture or are ready to experiment with dialogue in their piece, they need an expert to guide the way. You are the expert in your classroom. Invite students to have a peek inside your head as you deliberate over and expand upon an idea or reread and revise. To think aloud while writing, stop periodically to highlight your thought processes and make teaching points. Take this opportunity to explicitly show students how writers think strategically as they compose text. Students gain essential knowledge from demonstration lessons in which we model the author's craft (Fuhler & Walther, 2007).

Once you have demonstrated, children benefit from some shared or interactive writing experiences to further apply the skill or strategy alongside a mentor. After experiences such as these, students will be prepared to take the next steps. Whether they are working closely with a teacher in guided writing, developing ideas with a partner, or writing independently, children will be equipped to put pencil to paper with confidence, knowing that they have the background and support they need to succeed. To illustrate the gradual release of responsibility approach, we will define and describe each step of the process.

Modeled Writing

Children grow as writers when you model your writing on a regular basis. To explain, modeled writing serves the same purpose in the writing workshop as read-aloud/think-aloud does during a reading workshop. The act of modeling clarifies expectations of what writers will be doing on their own. As you write aloud, students see firsthand that writing is tricky and messy, not an easy step-by-step process. While you are in the process of composing, you may pause to think, reread, and revise. Students observe as you cross out words that don't make sense, replacing them with better choices, or chopping up words to spell them using the sounds you hear. Generally, this is not a

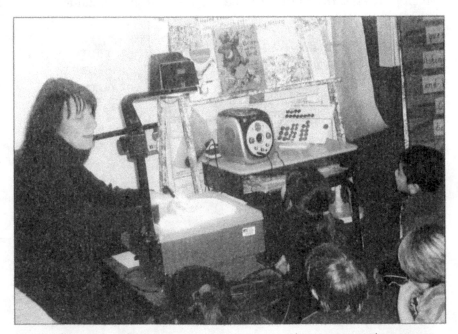

Notice the overhead projector is on a low cart so that we can gather our students around us as we model our writing.

time for student questions or input. We let our students know this by saying, "As I write, I'm going to share my thinking aloud. I know you are thoughtful students and will want to help me, but please don't raise your hand or interrupt. When I need your help, I'll ask, 'Can someone please give me a suggestion here?'"

The act of modeling also involves choosing where you record your modeled texts. Some teachers prefer chart paper, while others use the chalkboard. We usually write on an overhead projector positioned on a cart that sits low to the ground so that we can gather our writers around us on the floor. Of course, we have to set some guidelines about youngsters not sticking their hands in front of the light to create a puppet show while we are writing! Following our writing workshop mini-lesson, we either model or engage in a shared or interactive writing experience before sending children off to write. Following are a few tips to keep in mind as you model your own writing.

- Think aloud as you write, making your decision-making process visible. This is a habit that develops with time and practice.
- Reread, rethink, and revise as you go. Don't wait for the end of a piece to revise.
- Show writers that it is okay to let their ideas flow. Don't try to write with perfect handwriting, spelling, and grammar the first time.
- Stop in the middle of a piece. We've learned this technique from our students with special needs, who frequently have a difficult time with transitions. Pause to think about a typical day in your classroom. When we did this, we discovered that we regularly ask students to stop what they are doing when they are right in the middle because it's time to go to P.E., eat lunch, or switch to the next subject. But, do we model how to smoothly make this transition? Stopping in the middle of your piece shows students that the workshop is an ongoing event that will occur day after day. If you don't finish a piece on Monday, you can pick up where you left off on Tuesday and so on.
- Enjoy sharing your thoughts and ideas with your students. They love to hear what you have to say!

Shared Writing

Modeled writing places you in control of the ideas and content. To release responsibility to students, engage in shared writing experiences. Often, we use shared writing lessons to practice a specific aspect of writing, such as composing a story with a beginning, middle, and end, or creating a list of guidelines for the writing center. During shared writing, you will collaborate with your students to compose a text. You act as a scribe, eliciting input and suggestions while you continue to think aloud as you write. The focus of shared writing is on the composing process and on writing a text that children can later read. The emphasis is on the message or story. It is the ideal time to reinforce what you have demonstrated during modeled writing.

Interactive Writing

Interactive writing is similar to shared writing in that you work with your students to create a piece of writing. The difference is that while composing you select individual students to assist you in writing letters, words, or phrases, depending on their ability. Thus, you and your students write together using a "shared pen" (Fountas & Pinnell, 1996). "Interactive writing provides opportunities for teachers to engage in instruction precisely at the point of student need" (Button, Johnson, & Furgerson, 1996, p. 447) and to create conventional pieces of text for students to read and refer to at a later date. Here are some possible shared and interactive writing experiences:

- Revising and editing the morning message
- Writing about class experiences/activities
- Recording facts learned during science and social studies units
- Creating a story summary
- Composing big books
- Rewriting familiar texts
- Labeling graphs and charts

Depending on the focus of your mini-lesson and the needs of your learners, you may choose to engage your students in an interactive or

Key Steps in Shared and Interactive Writing

- ✦ Establish a purpose for writing.
- ✦ Brainstorm ideas for creating the text.
- ✦ Construct the text together (using a shared pen if it is an interactive writing experience).
- ✦ Reread, revise, and edit the text.
- ✦ Revisit the text and focus on key vocabulary words and phonetic features of individual words.
- ✦ Summarize and reflect on the learning that occurred.
- ✦ Extend the experience by placing the text in the classroom library for further enjoyment.

Giselle shares the chalk with her teacher during an interactive writing experience.

shared writing activity. Oftentimes, if the text you are composing is complex, it may take a day or so to complete. It is up to you to decide whether your students need the scaffolding and support such writing experiences provide before they are ready to move on to guided writing.

Guided Writing

At this point you may be asking, "What is guided writing, and where does it fit in the gradual release of responsibility model?" Because we support our students either in individual or small-group conferences, we view the portion of writing workshop where students are writing on their own as guided writing. Thus, we use many of the same techniques that we use during the guided reading portion of reading workshop when working with writers. For example, after our mini-lesson, we send students off to do their writing work. For more information on small-group conferring, see pages 28–29. As you have no doubt experienced, many students in your classroom need support and guidance to become independent writers. For that reason, it is helpful to group students with similar strengths or learning needs so you can offer this guidance in a manageable format. What does guided writing look like in our classrooms? See the chart of our expectations at right.

"Independent" Writing

In our classrooms, students have multiple opportunities to practice the craft of writing. One such opportunity is independent writing. You'll notice that we put the word *independent* in quotation marks, because nothing is truly independent in the primary grades! During independent writing, children have the chance to work alone and use their acquired knowledge of the writing process to compose and construct their own text (McCarrier, Pinnell, & Fountas, 2000). We offer students an independent writing opportunity each day during journal-writing time (see pages 25–26 for more on journal writing). This means we do not provide students with prompts or a mini-lesson

What Does Guided Writing Look Like?

- Students choosing their own perfect writing space (Note: Some students will require guidance to find an appropriate place.)

- Children writing individually, in pairs, triads, or small groups

- Teacher circulating or conferring with individuals or small groups

What Does Guided Writing Sound Like?

- A quiet buzz of writing-related discussions

- Students chopping up or stretching out (sounding out) words for writing

- Students rereading texts to figure out what to write next, to listen for fluency, to revise, and to edit

prior to writing, but we certainly provide a lot of help, encouragement, and assistance while they are writing. Another opportunity for independent writing may occur in a writing center, where students work with peers while you are busy working with individuals or small groups on focused reading instruction.

WHEN TO TEACH

Without a doubt, your teaching days are as jam-packed as ours. See the sample schedule on page 23. That is why the last aspect of balanced writing instruction is the most challenging. We've seen from our extensive work with teachers that most of us understand the "what" and the "how" of writing instruction. It's fitting it all into our busy day that becomes prob-

Journal time offers students an opportunity to independently use their knowledge of the writing craft.

lematic. We simply can't stretch the day to include one more thing. Honestly, that was one of our motivating factors in writing this book. We wanted to create a plan to help teachers fit it all in.

Sample Schedule for Writing Workshop or "Writing Time" in Half-Day Kindergarten

Monday	Tuesday	Wednesday	Thursday	Friday
Read Aloud Like a Writer	Morning Message	Mini-Lesson	Morning Message	Read Aloud Like a Writer
Shared Writing	Journal	Guided Writing	Journal	Class Book

	MONDAY	TUESDAY	WEDNESDAY	THURSDAY	FRIDAY
			Sample Daily Schedule		
8:50–9:10	Book Exchange/ Independent Reading	Independent Reading	Book Exchange/ Independent Reading	Independent Reading	Book Exchange/ Independent Reading
9:10–9:35	Weekend Share/Journal	Morning Message, Poem, Read-Aloud	Morning Message, Poem, Read-Aloud	Morning Message, Poem, Read-Aloud	Morning Message, Poem, Read-Aloud
9:35–10:05	Morning Message, Poem, Read-Aloud	Journal	Journal	Journal	Journal
10:05–10:50	Writing Workshop SNACK	Reading Workshop SNACK	Reading Workshop SNACK	Writing Workshop SNACK	Reading Workshop SNACK
10:50–11:20	P.E.	Word Study	ART	MUSIC	P.E.
11:20–11:45	Reading Workshop	MUSIC	ART	P.E.	Writing Workshop
11:45–12:30		Writing Workshop	Writing Workshop	Word Study	Word Study (12:00–12:30)
12:30–1:10	LUNCH	LUNCH	LUNCH	LUNCH	LUNCH
1:15–1:30	Read-Aloud	Read-Aloud	Read-Aloud	Read-Aloud	Read-Aloud
1:30–2:15	Word Study	Calendar, Thinking Journal, Math	Calendar, Thinking Journal, Math	Calendar, Thinking Journal, Math	Calendar, Thinking Journal, Math
2:15–2:30	RECESS	RECESS	RECESS	RECESS	RECESS
2:30–3:20	Science/ Social Studies	Science/ Social Studies	Word Study	Science/ Social Studies	Science/ Social Studies

Morning Message

We're sure that many of you are familiar with a morning message. Some refer to it as "daily news," while others call it a "writing warm-up." To clarify, a morning message is simply a short text written to, with, or by your students. We both choose to write our message on the chalkboard each day. You may prefer using chart paper to provide a written record of the learning that has occurred. The beauty of the morning message is that it takes only 5 to 15 minutes of instructional time each day, but when you multiply the minutes by the total days in school, it computes to an abundant amount of time demonstrating, talking, and thinking about writing. We have both used a morning message as part of our daily writing instruction for years. Luckily, we have also helped each other learn how to use it to its fullest potential. In this book you will find messages that will heighten students' awareness of different writing genres, explore various aspects of conventions, and illuminate other facets of the craft of writing.

The morning message is written to, with, or by students.

Morning Message Steps

1. Pre-write a message or compose a message in a shared or interactive writing format.

2. Using a pointer, point to the words as you chorally read the message.

3. To complete, revise, or edit the message, invite students to the chalkboard or chart to help. You may want to have a small container of chalk or markers handy for easy access. To increase participation, set the guideline that each student only gets one opportunity per day to assist at the board. Others can answer questions as you discuss and make teaching points. Vary students from day to day so all learners get frequent chances to participate.

4. Once the message is complete, reread with fluency and expression. This is a habit you want to instill early on!

Journal Writing

To journal or not to journal, that is the question! We debate this quandary year after year and always decide to offer students a regular opportunity to write in their journals. We don't do a mini-lesson before journal, but we do follow up with sharing. Since this is an essential part of our balanced writing instruction, we will describe our journal writing practice by answering some frequently asked questions. As always, remember there is no right way to do journals as long as your students are writing, writing, writing!

Why do you choose to do a journal *and* writing workshop?

We choose to do both because the journal provides a short, focused piece of writing that we can read each day. We believe it is important for students to orally reread what they have written. When children read their journals to us, we offer specific, individualized feedback to help them grow as writers.

What do your students' journals look like?

The students get a different journal for each month, and they change throughout the year. We make their journals out of copy paper with a construction paper cover and back. Their first journal is a half-sheet format without lines, to accommodate the needs of students who are doing more drawing than writing. As the year progresses, we add lines according to the students' writing ability. This is different every year! The writing lines we have created are provided in appendices A1–A2 on pages 171–172.

How do students use the editing checklists?

If we could teach students one thing as writers, it would be to reread their written work with a careful eye on the details. The editing checklist (included in appendices A1–A2) is a reminder to students to reread and edit their writing for specific conventions. The conventions listed at the bottom of the checklist are driven by your expectations and by what you know students can successfully fix. It is the students' responsibility to hunt for errors. The checklist, coupled with a quick glance from you to see if they truly did it (or just checked the boxes!), will promote student self-checking.

Do you give students topics or prompts?

No, we choose not to do this. Instead we make an effort to model and discuss different ideas they can write about in their journals. We do much of this teaching during the morning message.

How long does journal writing take each day?

The students write for about 15 to 20 minutes. During this time, we begin by working with our struggling writers. After we help them get started, we call students over by groups to read their journals to us. We point out the exciting things each student did in his or her journal and make a quick teaching point.

Do students share their journals with the class?

Yes. We use craft sticks with students' names printed on them and choose three to four sticks a day. Selected students share their journals with the class while the other children listen, ask two "detail" questions, and then share any compliments they have for the writers.

Do you send their journals home?
At the end of each month we send students' journals home with a note to return when ready (the note appears on Appendix A3, page 173). Once they're returned, we keep all of their journals and use them for ongoing assessment, report cards, and conferences. At the end of the year we celebrate our writing accomplishments by having a Journal Party!

A Balanced Writing Workshop

Writing workshop. For some of us, those two simple words cause stress and anxiety. We've read the books and

Students celebrate a successful year of writing during their Journal Party.

watched the videotaped lessons, but somehow when we try the same things with our students, it does not go quite as smoothly as we imagined. The books never talk about the child with autism or the learner who has an attention span of about 15 seconds. How do you manage a writing workshop and meet their needs? Over the years we've encountered the same struggles, and we have developed some strategies that we think you may find helpful.

To begin, we know that student choice is an essential element of the writing workshop. However, the reality of teaching today is that we must also find time for students to practice working with the genres and organizational structures that will help them to succeed on school-based writing tasks such as standardized tests. To accomplish both, we balance our workshop time between student choice and teacher-guided writing opportunities. For example, most often our mini-lessons are designed to illuminate and explore an aspect of writing craft. They end with an open-ended invitation for students to experiment with that aspect in their ongoing pieces. Occasionally, mini-lessons may lead to a specific type of writing such as those found in the genre explorations or to guided practice of one of the components of balanced writing. In that case, we guide students to make a choice within the structure we provide. For instance, the mini-lessons might teach students how to write a friendly letter, organize an expository paragraph, or pen a poem. When this happens, we typically provide students with specially designed booklets or writing paper.

Below, we've provided some questions for you to ponder as you think about your writing workshop and prepare to establish routines and procedures. We will attempt to answer some of these questions in the upcoming chapters in a feature called Writing Workshop Tip.

- Where will students record their written work?

- What other supplies are needed? Where will students get these supplies?

- Where will their finished pieces of writing be stored?

- What are your guidelines for writing workshop time?

  * Do you want to begin the writing time with five minutes of silent writing?

  * How will students ask for help?

  * How will you confer with students?

  * If you are conferring and students need help, what do they do?

  * What do they do when they finish a piece?

  * How often will children publish a piece of writing?

Mini-Lessons

Mini-lessons are focused, intentional, and explicit opportunities to teach the various aspects of the writer's craft. They typically occur at the beginning of the workshop but can easily take place when you are working with a small group, during a conference, or any time children are writing. Effective writing mini-lessons should be brief, allowing time afterwards for students to write. They should also include the following:

- Authentic writing tips driven by the needs of your young writers. Ask yourself, "What do my students need at this time to continue writing well?"

The Components of a Primary Writing Workshop

5–15 minutes: Read Like a Writer

When reading mentor texts or student work samples:

- Notice and name writing techniques.

- Illuminate the traits of good writing.

- Develop an understanding of a specific genre.

- Analyze and evaluate written work.

5–15 minutes: Mini-Lesson and Teacher Modeling

- Explicitly teach writing skills, strategies, or procedures determined by ongoing student assessment.

- Routinely model and think aloud while writing or work with students on a shared or interactive writing experience.

15–30 minutes: Writing

Children write while you confer with individuals or meet with small groups.

5–10 minutes: Sharing

Students share individually, in partners, or in small groups.

- A clear, focused objective. Ask yourself, "What is the point of this lesson? What do I want my students to get out of it?"
- An example to show students what you are talking about. Specific examples can come from carefully selected books, student writing samples, or teacher modeling.
- An invitation to try something new in their writing. Mini-lessons are not usually followed by some kind of work or "guided practice." We must trust that our writers will try things out when they are ready (Ray & Laminack, 2001; Routman, 2005).

Guided Writing Groups: A Time-Efficient Approach to Conferences

As we shared earlier, we structure our writing workshop in the same way we organize our reading workshop. We launch each workshop with a read-aloud and a whole-class mini-lesson to focus on a specific strategy or skill. The mini-lesson leads to a demonstration and then independent practice time. In the case of a reading workshop, students are reading independently, with partners, or with us in small groups. Likewise, during the writing workshop, students are writing. Some days we spend quite a bit of time "honeybee" conferencing (Farris, 2005, p. 337). Simply put, we are buzzing around like crazy, helping those writers who need support, and, depending on the year, that could include half of our class!

The Components of the Mini-Lessons Found in This Book

Preparation: Consult this section while writing your lesson plans to find any books or materials you may need to gather to do the mini-lesson. Most often, you will not have enough time in one writing workshop to complete the entire mini-lesson, especially if you are planning to read and discuss the techniques students notice in the book. A time-saving idea you might consider is reading the book prior to writing workshop so that during your mini-lesson you can reread selected sections, and then chart or discuss your findings to illuminate the writer's craft.

Explanation: The explanation that will appear in this section is for you, not for your students. We will give you a glimpse into our thinking by answering the key questions "What is the point of this mini-lesson?" and "What do I want my students to learn from it?"

Demonstration: A few tips for teacher modeling will be included in the demonstration portion of the lesson.

Invitation: Because students need time to apply what they have learned in mini-lessons to their own writing, each mini-lesson should conclude with an invitation. We will write this invitation in kid-friendly language to help guide your teaching.

Other days, we confer with students in small groups that are comparable to guided reading groups. How does this work? Once students are settled and writing, we assemble a small group of children based on their needs. We meet in a centrally located place in our room. The groups are informal and flexible, and they change often. In fact, we may call students over to join us in the middle of a conference if they look like they need some help. Depending on the ability of the group, we may revisit or extend the content of the mini-lesson, have students voice questions and interact with one another, or guide students individually while the others continue writing. There are many advantages to this arrangement. Keeping the routines and structures parallel in your reading and writing workshops helps students to become independent readers and writers. Having a group gathered around and chatting with one student at a time is quicker than calling students over one by one.

Publishing and Celebrating

We wholeheartedly agree with Katie Wood Ray and Lisa Cleaveland (2004) when they assert that asking students to reproduce their written work in the name of publishing it just doesn't make sense. Sometimes we get so caught up in the publishing phase of the writing process we neglect the work that builds strong writers, such as prewriting, drafting, and revising. Not everything children write will be published. In fact, Regie Routman's wise words have helped us quite a bit. She contends that "If you're reading everything your students write, they're not writing enough" (2005, p. 65).

During the writing workshop we want students to spend time writing. Occasionally, we will encourage children to present and celebrate their finished work in creative ways. At the end of a genre exploration they may simply polish and present. For our students, that means that after revising and editing their finished pieces, they carefully illustrate a construction paper cover, staple it on their written work, and proudly parade around the room. Another option for sharing finished work is an author's circle (see guidelines at right).

About one time each quarter we provide students with the opportunity to have a special piece published with our "Parent Publishing Company." To create a parent publishing company, we recruit willing parents early in the school year. These parents volunteer to type students' work at home. To guide their work, we send home the note found in Appendix A3 on page 173.

> ## Student Guidelines for Small-Group Author's Circles
>
> ✦ Practice reading aloud before joining the author's circle.
>
> ✦ If your text is long, pick your favorite part.
>
> ✦ Take turns.
>
> ✦ Listen carefully to the author who is sharing.
>
> ✦ Point out a specific trait or feature of their writing. Begin with "I noticed that you . . . ."

HOW TO ASSESS

We believe the purpose of assessment is twofold. First, assessment helps to focus instruction on the needs of students. When we identify what our young writers know and are able to do, we can design lessons that will nudge them further. Along with focusing instruction, assessment helps guide students as they learn to look at their own work with critical eyes. Meaningful self-assessment begins by helping children understand the complex craft of writing. You might consider creating a "What Writers Do" chart similar to the one found on page 31.

Celebrate Writing!

Each time students complete a piece of writing, choose a different way to share and celebrate.

Family Feedback Send the child's piece home with a blank sheet labeled Family Feedback attached to the back. Family members write positive comments.

Cross-Age Buddies Partner with an upper-grade class and meet periodically to share writing.

Sharing Chair Use a microphone (we both have small karaoke machines in our classrooms) when students are reading their piece aloud to the class. It makes the listening experience enjoyable for all!

Famous Author Basket Store finished work in a folder labeled "Writing Portfolio" in a basket marked "Famous [Kindergarten, First-, or Second-Grade] Authors." The students reach for these on a regular basis.

Writing Workshop Celebration End the year with a celebration! Provide time for students to share favorite pieces with one another. If students are willing, ask them to donate a piece to your collection for use as a mentor text for future students.

While sharing, use a microphone to amplify students' voices.

So how do we select writing assessments that are both meaningful and manageable? For the most part, we use teacher observation and anecdotal assessment data to drive our instructional decisions. We carefully observe our students as we engage in whole-class conversations, confer with students in small groups, and meet with writers individually to read and discuss their work. We jot quick notes on a grid sheet stored on a clipboard. Our anecdotal notes guide us as we plan our lessons or select students for small-group instruction. To help organize our notes we use a quick and clever method shared by our colleague Jennifer Kroll. Once we've collected anecdotal data on all of our writers, we divide a blank sheet of paper into four

> ## What Writers Do
>
> **Writers Read**
>
> - Read a lot of books.
> - Reread your writing aloud.
> - Read the writing of your classmates.
>
> **Writers Think**
>
> - Be on the lookout for ideas.
> - Write with a purpose in mind.
> - Reread, revise, and refine as you go.
>
> **Writers Communicate**
>
> - Write to your audience.
> - Edit your work so others can read it.
> - Discuss your writing with others.

sections. We label each section with a target skill, and then list students who need further teaching or enrichment in that specific area. We refer to this sheet often during writing workshop. (See example on next page.)

In addition to our ongoing anecdotal notes, each month we take a closer look at each student's independent writing using the Journal Writing Observations chart that appears in Appendix A4 on page 174. Finally, near the end of each grading period, we take a sample of the students' writing and assess it using a developmental continuum found in the following resources:

6+1 Traits of Writing: The Complete Guide for the Primary Grades (Culham, 2005)
Creating Young Writers (Spandel, 2008)
Seeing With New Eyes: Using the 6 + 1 Trait Writing Model (Bellamy, 2005)

Final Thoughts

We're hopeful this chapter gave you the foundation you need to meet the challenge of teaching writing. We've packed each chapter that follows with ideas and resources to guide you in the decision-making process of planning writing instruction that will inspire your students to become engaged, thoughtful, and passionate writers.

Anecdotal Notes

1. Katie *labored writing* *detailed, expressive* *illustrations* *unique ideas* *pre-phonetic speller*	**2. Lenny** *limited topics* *attempting* *conventions* *transitional speller*	**3. Moriah** *begins pieces with* *original ideas* *has difficulty with* *middle and end* *phonetic speller*	**4. Dan** *needs 1:1 assistance* *to sustain* *independent writing* *unique ideas* *pre-phonetic speller*
5. Jordan *a lot to share* *during whole class* *conversations* *spends much of* *writing time* *"thinking" about* *ideas*	**6. Jake** *able to write* *quickly and fluently* *repeats similar* *ideas* *transitional speller*	**7. Brynne** *varied topics* *unique voice* *uses a variety of* *conventions* *transitional speller*	**8. Robert** *varied topics* *detailed illustrations* *advanced knowledge* *of conventions* *conventional* *speller*
9. Chelsea *needs 1:1* *assistance to* *match letters/* *sounds* *illustrations* *contain voice*	**10. Larry** *limited ideas* *writing seems* *labored* *advanced use of* *conventions* *transitional speller*	**11. Jennifer** *ideas are original* *but conventions* *of writing make it* *difficult to read* *voice-filled* *illustrations*	**12. Matt** *varied topics* *creative writer* *writes easily* *transitional speller*

Small-Group Planning Sheet

Strategies for Developmental Spelling Katie, Chelsea, Dan, Jennifer	Idea Development Lenny, Larry, Jordan
The students in this group have a wealth of ideas but lack sound-letter knowledge or attention to task to put their thoughts into written words.	*This is the "I don't have any ideas!" group. We'll talk about their interests and backgrounds to uncover ideas for writing.*
Elaboration Moriah, Jake	**Enrichment of Ideas/Writing Techniques** Brynne, Robert, Matt
This is the "I'm done!" group. The students have the ability to elaborate and add details; they simply need encouragement to apply their talents.	*This group quickly picks up on the techniques and ideas shared in mentor texts and mini-lessons and can learn from each other as they write.*

Use information from anecdotal notes to form temporary small groups.

Chapter 2

September: Setting the Stage

Ahhh! September

Summer has slipped by, and, after countless hours of preparation, you are ready to greet your fresh-faced students. It doesn't take long to resume the frantic pace and experience the joys and challenges of September in the primary grades. As the year begins anew, we reminisce about our class at the end of the previous year. Remember giving directions once and having everyone (well, almost everyone) follow them? Now we return to spelling out each procedure step by step. Luckily, we know how critical the first days and weeks are to establishing routines and setting the stage for a productive year of learning. With this in mind, we patiently model and teach the behaviors we want our young learners to employ, often repeating ourselves over and over and over again. The same holds true for the first month of writing instruction.

September is spent purposefully building a solid foundation for a year of writing experiences while at the same time showing students how writers think, act, and work. As a wise teacher, you know that each lesson you teach at the beginning of the year is as much about setting expectations for myriad behaviors as it is about teaching the content. Furthermore, each time a student draws or writes you have an opportunity to learn about that child's strengths and needs. In order for all of your writers to have a successful year, you build on their strengths and provide personalized instruction to improve their weaknesses, just as Ms. McCaw does for Dudley in *Ms. McCaw Learns to Draw* (Zemach, 2008). This picture book is a must-read because it helps students understand that every child has unique talents and abilities.

Part 1: Morning Message Ideas and Samples

You will find that most of the morning message ideas for September are designed for you to write prior to the students' arrival. As you are well aware, the attention span of young students in September is short. Prewriting the message with a specific purpose in mind allows more time during the message lesson to make teaching points and elicit discussion. When appropriate, invite students to assist in editing the messages to keep the pace quick and the interest high. Depending on the needs of your students, you may consider repeating a message type for a few days or even a week, alternating among messages, or saving the ideas for later in the school year.

MORNING MESSAGE IDEA: WHAT DO YOU NOTICE?

Use this message to informally assess students' awareness of concepts of print and other language-related knowledge. Prewrite a message about the upcoming day's activities. Begin by asking, "Does anyone notice anything in the message today? You might notice a letter you recognize, an interesting word, a number, a punctuation mark, or some words that look the same." For instance, in the sample message, one student may notice that the words *exciting* and *interesting* end in the same fashion, while

> **Morning Message Sample**
>
> ### What Do You Notice?
>
> Good morning! Welcome to first grade. We are going to have an exciting and interesting year together. SMILE and MAKE GOOD CHOICES!

another child might remark that some words are written in all capital letters. Both observations will lead you to meaningful discussions about words and the choices authors make while writing. To encourage noticing, invite students to raise hands, individually come to the board or chart, tell the class what they've noticed, and mark it in some way. You can use a message similar to this throughout the year to highlight specific word patterns, conventions, sentence parts, or other language concepts you wish to emphasize.

Morning Message: What Do You Notice?

MORNING MESSAGE IDEA: SEPTEMBER WORD CHART

Each month, in addition to teaching students how to spell grade-appropriate high-frequency words, invite learners to help you create a list of seasonal or curricular-related words during morning message. Collect the words on chart paper that you can later display in your room. To aid students in locating the words in the days to come, consider writing each word in a different color or drawing a picture next to each word. For second-grade writers, take a digital photograph of the list, add

Morning Message Sample		
September Word Chart		
school	read	lunch
bus	write	pencil
teacher	recess	friend
principal	Labor Day	learn

some blank spaces for students to write their own personal words, and then make copies for students to store in an accessible spot such as their writing workshop folder.

MORNING MESSAGE IDEA: LOOKING AT LETTERS

To support young writers as they begin to distinguish between capital and lowercase letters, prewrite a message alternating between uppercase and lowercase letters. After reading the entire message aloud with your students, begin to rewrite the message, spelling out each word as you write. Invite students to clap each time they see a capital letter in the middle of a word. To make this

Morning Message Sample
Looking at Letters
GoOd mORNing! Do YOu NOTICe anyTHing strangE in OUR mESSage todAY?

an interactive writing experience, select individuals to share the chalk or marker and rewrite a word or two along the way.

MORNING MESSAGE IDEA: SPACES BETWEEN WORDS 🔘

Many young children who are beginning to write words find it difficult to leave appropriate spacing between the words. For most students, this skill improves with time and practice. To help students remember to leave spaces between words as they write, demonstrate how to place a

> **Morning Message Sample**
>
> ### Spaces Between Words
>
> Goodmorningbrainystudents!
> Thebreezeischillytoday.
> Didyouwearajacket?

Morning Message: Spaces Between Words

craft stick between words as a tactile cue to move their pencil over before writing the next word. For this demonstration, allow ample room below the message to rewrite the same words with spaces in between, or simply draw lines between the words, reread, and invite students to clap each time a word ends.

MORNING MESSAGE IDEA: WHERE DO THE PERIODS GO? 🔘

Before novice writers develop the concept of a sentence, they have a difficult time determining where to place the ending punctuation. Typically, they place punctuation at the end of every word or line instead of at the end of each complete sentence. To develop students' awareness of proper placement of punctuation, begin by reading the message the way it is currently punctuated (see sample). Point out that the period "signals" (Rickards & Hawes, 2006) the reader to stop. Students will often giggle as you read because it sounds so silly. Continue the demonstration by editing the message with students' help, showing them how to move the ending punctuation and insert

> **Morning Message Sample**
>
> ### Where Do the Periods Go?
>
> Today is a busy.
> day we have a lot.
> of exciting things.
> planned i can't.
> wait to get started.

appropriate capital letters. When you reread the sentences with proper punctuation, include an auditory signal for a period, such as a clicker or bell.

MORNING MESSAGE IDEA: THINK SMALL!

When telling or writing about experiences, youngsters frequently regale their readers with a "bed-to-bed" story. For example, when writing about their favorite birthday present they begin with, "I woke up. I ate breakfast. I got dressed. It was time for my birthday party. . ." By the time they reach the exciting part, they are tired of writing! For this reason, writers need to learn how to "think small"—in other words, how to focus on one aspect of an event or happening. Try this message to get writers thinking about specific moments instead of writing about the entire day. If you write this message on chart paper, you will be able to preserve it for further discussions about this topic.

MORNING MESSAGE IDEA: WORD EXCHANGE

One important aspect of writing is choosing precise words to communicate ideas to your reader. Each time you present a vocabulary lesson, you are teaching young children about word choice. In addition, you strengthen students' word choice as you read aloud and discuss key words in the text. A quick and easy way to broaden your students' writing vocabularies is to introduce them to different words in the morning message. To prepare for

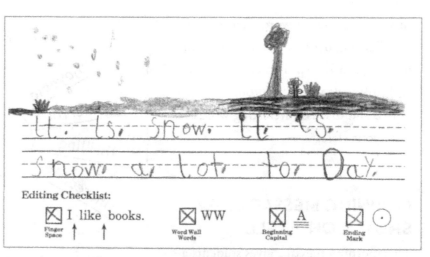

A novice writer places punctuation at the end of every word.

Morning Message Sample

Think Small!

If you were writing about a birthday party, what moments could you describe?

Birthday Party Moments (possible responses): blowing out the candles, opening gifts, eating the cake, playing games

Morning Message Sample

Let's make a word exchange! What are other words that mean the same as FUN?

this message, select words that students are choosing over and over again. This message can be repeated each month with different words to prompt you to notice and discuss interesting words with your class.

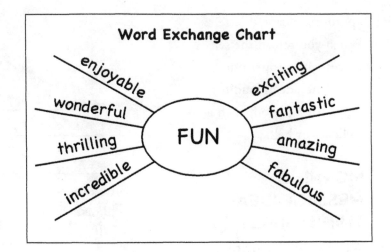

MORNING MESSAGE IDEA: SHOW, DON'T TELL

This morning message gives students a glimpse into the difference between words that show and words that tell. Many primary writers tend to tell how they are feeling rather than *showing* the reader with vivid verbs and description. To introduce this message, invite a student to act out an emotion such as angry or happy. Jot down the verbs that describe what the child is doing. The sample includes a few sentences to get you started—we're sure you and your students will come up with many more. A book that ties in nicely with this message is *On Monday When It Rained* (Kachenmeister, 2001).

> **Morning Message Sample**
>
> **Show, Don't Tell**
>
> Which sentences show you how the boy is feeling?
> The boy is happy. The smiling boy jumps and cheers.
> He stomped his feet as he walked away. The boy is mad.
> The boy is sad. The tears rolled down his face.

MORNING MESSAGE IDEA: NOUNS ALL AROUND

Use this message after the mini-lesson on page 46 to reinforce the concept of nouns.

> **Morning Message Sample**
>
> **Nouns All Around**
>
> Can you circle the nouns in this message?
>
> The door flew open and out darted
> my puppy. My sister chased him for
> miles. Finally, Sarah found Beanie
> hiding at the park.

MORNING MESSAGE IDEA: THE LETTER STEALER—CONSONANTS

While writing a message, leave out consonants, vowels, blends, digraphs, or other phonetic elements addressed during your word study lessons. We tell our children that the "letter stealer" visited. Students enjoy helping to fill in the missing letters. The first time we share this message, we focus on consonant sounds. But you'll see that this message appears in each chapter to help you reinforce student learning of various phonetic elements.

> **Morning Message Sample**
>
> ### The Letter Stealer— Consonants
>
> Good rainy ___orning!
> So__ething is ___issing in our ___essage. What is it??

MORNING MESSAGE IDEA: LET'S SORT

To introduce the concept of organization, we offer students opportunities to sort ideas or concepts into various categories. To facilitate sorting, place a pocket chart near your meeting area and write each word on a separate index card. This message presents limitless possibilities for students to share their individual thinking about sorting or organizing. You may want to choose words that are related to a specific content area in your curriculum to reinforce vocabulary knowledge.

> **Morning Message Sample**
>
> ### Let's Sort
>
> How would you sort these words? Why?
>
> pencil, teacher, principal, eraser, classroom, gym, nurse, scissors, markers, secretary, librarian, lunchroom, library

MORNING MESSAGE IDEA: MIXED-UP NAMES

If your students had difficulty discriminating between capital and lowercase letters in the Looking at Letters message on page 35, try this message. Write the students' names using uppercase letters in the middle as pictured in the sample at right. Invite each child to join you at the board and rewrite his or her name so that only the first letter is capitalized.

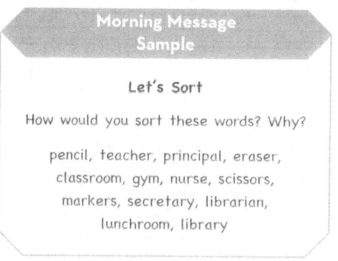

Read-Alouds for Writers		
Title and Author	**Brief Summary**	**Focus**
39 Uses for a Friend (Ziefert, 2001)	Brief text and simple illustrations celebrate the many ways friends help each other.	Ideas
The Adventures of Taxi Dog (Barracca & Barracca, 1990)	The taxi dog tales are written with an inviting rhyming text. If the children enjoy the first book, try *Maxi, The Hero* (1991) and *Maxi, The Star* (1993).	Sentence Fluency
Max's Dragon (Banks, 2008)	In the sequel to *Max's Words* (2006), Max searches for rhyming words while playing with his imaginary dragon.	Word Choice
Ms. McCaw Learns to Draw (Zemach, 2008)	When Ms. McCaw is unable to draw a face, she enlists the help of Dudley, a student for whom school is difficult.	Setting the Stage: Accepting Different Learning Styles
The Name Quilt (Root, 2003)	Sadie loves to listen to her grandma tell family stories about the relatives named on a quilt.	Ideas
A Quiet Place (Wood, 2002)	Using his imagination, a child explores quiet places alive with adventure.	Reading-Writing Connection
Read All About It! (Bush & Bush, 2008)	Tyrone, a reluctant reader, meets his match when he steps into Ms. Libro's homeroom.	Reading-Writing Connection
Things That Are Most in the World (Barrett, 1998)	Readers discover the quietest, silliest, and hottest things in the world. Includes a ready-to-use class book page!	Ideas
We All Go Traveling By (Roberts, 2003)	Sing about all the different ways children travel to school.	Sentence Fluency
Wild About Books (Sierra, 2004)	A librarian named Molly McGrew introduces the animals to the joys of reading and writing.	Reading-Writing Connection

Part 2: A Menu of Mini-Lessons—Establishing Routines and Exploring the Concepts of Writing

The main goal of the September mini-lessons is to create a community of learners who understand the work of the writer. We've designed the first mini-lessons to help you introduce writers to the components of balanced writing instruction while at the same time giving them a glimpse into the writing world. Each time you gather your young writers around for a mini-lesson, you are establishing routines and procedures. As you read and discuss books, you are helping students learn the manners involved in participating in a class conversation. We know that the month of September is a hectic and exhausting time. For that reason, you'll find the September mini-lessons short, direct, and to the point. We've also kept them to a minimum, because many can be repeated again and again. Keep in mind as you continue that, depending on your class and the time you've allotted for writing workshop, you may need a day or two to complete a mini-lesson. It is more important that your students have ample time to write each day than it is that you finish an entire lesson at once. Take your time and enjoy getting to know your writers.

> ### WRITING WORKSHOP TIP: Where Will Students Record Their Written Work?
>
> Here are two ideas that may work for you and your students. For many young writers, beginning the year with pre-stapled booklets made of plain copy paper offers a familiar book-like format for writing. The booklets can be either the full 8½ x 11 size or, to save paper, cut into half pages before stapling. These "mini-books" can be anywhere from three to ten pages in length. Later in the year, you may choose to have students transition to a writer's notebook to store their ongoing pieces of writing. We've included examples of writer's notebook paper in Appendix A5 on page 175. Notice there is space between the lines for revising. To store students' ongoing work, we use a two-pocket folder.

MINI-LESSON: LET YOUR IDEAS FLOW! 🔊

PREPARATION: Read and discuss *Ish* (Reynolds, 2004). After Ramon's brother criticizes his drawings, his sister helps him understand that his "ish" (tree-ish, house-ish, boat-ish) drawings are just perfect!

EXPLANATION: This lesson helps set the stage for writing. It gives children permission to make approximations in both their pictures and words. It sends the message that your classroom is a place where they can take risks and that you view mistakes as learning opportunities.

DEMONSTRATION: As you model, you will want students to understand the connection between spoken words and written words. You might begin by saying something like, "Today I'm going to let my ideas flow. I'll draw and write about something I want to tell you because that's what writers do."

INVITATION: "Authors, it's time to write. As you write, think about Ramon in the story we just read, and remember that 'ish' is okay in our classroom. Let your ideas flow!"

MINI-LESSON: WRITING IS HARD WORK! 🔵

PREPARATION: Read a book or discuss the challenges of being an author. Select from the following titles.

Author: A True Story (Lester, 1997). The author of the Tacky the Penguin series describes her challenges as a young writer and her continued struggles as an adult writer.

You Have to Write (Wong, 2002). Janet Wong's poetic language encourages children to see that their lives are filled with experiences about which to write. This book is more appropriate for second grade and beyond.

EXPLANATION: Early in the year, we stress the fact that daily writing time is a precious commodity. Students know that writers use their time wisely because writing is hard work.

DEMONSTRATION: Before writing, discuss how writers, just like readers, practice every day because being a writer takes hard work and practice. Remind students that they will have time to write each day during writing workshop. One of our goals for young writers is that they learn to reread their writing, evaluating and revising as they go. To reinforce this important writing skill, reread the work you did the day before, revise as needed, and then continue. You may want to restate, "Authors draw or write about something that they want to tell others. Today I want to tell you more about _____. Listen as I write down what I think by listening to the sounds in each word and writing the letters that match each sound." Depending on the writing ability of your class, you may be drawing a picture, then labeling it with words, writing a sentence or two, or penning a paragraph. Your modeling should nudge students to challenge themselves and show them what is possible.

INVITATION: "Authors, I bet you are ready to get started. It's time to write more about something you know."

MINI-LESSON: WRITERS GET IDEAS FROM THEIR LIVES

PREPARATION: Read a book that demonstrates that writers get ideas from everyday events in their lives. Here are three titles to consider.

Arthur Writes a Story (Brown, 1996). Marc Brown's book works well for this lesson because Arthur begins writing his story about an event in his life, but then strays away from what he knows and ends up with a crazy, mixed-up piece. Mr. Ratburn helps Arthur understand the importance of writing about ideas that are close to his heart.

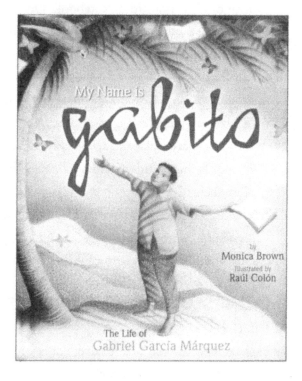

Mr. Putter and Tabby Write the Book (Rylant, 2004). On a snowy day Mr. Putter sets out to write a mystery novel, but after much deliberation ends up writing about something he knows—good things!

My Name is Gabito: The Life of Gabriel García Márquez (Brown, 2007). An inspiring biography of the Nobel Prize-winning novelist who got his ideas from his imagination, from the people he met, and from the things he saw.

EXPLANATION: The aim of this lesson is to encourage young writers to look at their world with writers' eyes, to see that their everyday experiences are possible writing topics. This lesson is the first step in guiding students to pick their own topics.

DEMONSTRATION: Discuss that writers often write about familiar topics. You can use either Arthur or Mr. Putter as an example. They both had more success writing about something they had experienced. Together with your class, brainstorm a list of topics that your students know a lot about. Topics may include favorite colors, favorite foods, family, pets, vacation, friends, school, and so on. You may continue to revise the chart throughout the year, adding topics of interest to your students. As always, continue your demonstration by modeling your own writing.

INVITATION: "Writers, if you are stuck and can't think of anything to write about today, take a look at our list of topics—it may spark an idea to get you started. Remember to reread your work before you begin."

MINI-LESSON: CREATING AN IDEA NOTEBOOK 🌓 🌎

PREPARATION:

- Copy one Idea Notebook for each student from appendix A6 on pages 176–178.
- Read and discuss *There's a Big, Beautiful World Out There!* (Carlson, 2004)

EXPLANATION: In addition to or instead of a topic list, another possibility for having students gather a bank of ideas is an Idea Notebook. Once students are familiar with the format, they can add ideas to their notebook during writing workshop.

DEMONSTRATION: Following a quick discussion about the book, begin your demonstration with, "Today I'm going to begin an Idea Notebook. This is a special place to record my ideas for writing." Show students how to write and/or draw their ideas.

INVITATION: "Authors, today we are going to work together to complete the first page of your Idea Notebook. Once you complete this page, you may choose to continue working in your Idea Notebook or continue your writing from yesterday."

MINI-LESSON: CHOP IT UP! INTRODUCING DEVELOPMENTAL SPELLING 🔵

PREPARATION: Gather a list of decodable words. It might include:

expand	*plastic*	*catalog*	*compact*
conflict	*frantic*	*habitat*	*fantastic*
instruct	*compliment*	*defender*	*quiver*

EXPLANATION: As we explained in Chapter 1, Words for Writers lessons help students build agency and independence as authors. Each time we model our own writing, discuss word patterns or families, or practice reading and spelling high-frequency words, we are teaching children about words for writers. This focused mini-lesson adds to the wealth of word knowledge your students are gathering from all the phonemic awareness, phonics, and word study lessons and activities you already incorporate into your daily instruction.

DEMONSTRATION: Begin with an explanation such as, "Today before I continue my writing, I want to think about what writers do when they have to spell a word." Begin with a word on your list. Say the word as you normally would. Next, say it phoneme by phoneme as you make a chopping motion with your two hands together. When students chop words, you want to make sure they are chopping from left to right, just as they will be writing the letters. Ask students to help you write the letters that match the sounds you hear. Continue in the same fashion with a few more words, and then resume your modeling.

INVITATION: "Smart spellers, while you are writing, don't forget to chop your words. That's what writers do."

MINI-LESSON: SHOWING FEELINGS IN YOUR WRITING

PREPARATION: Select and read a book about feelings. Here are two to consider.

My Many Colored Days (Seuss, 1996). From the archives of the late Dr. Seuss comes this book about a child whose moods are depicted as colorful animals.

Yesterday I Had the Blues (Frame, 2003). In this rhythmic tale, an African American boy describes his moods and the moods of his family. He explains that Daddy's got the grays and Gram's got the yellows. Enjoy a rainbow of colors and feelings as you read this energetic book.

EXPLANATION: One concrete way to explain the concept of voice to your students is by relating voice to feelings. After reading a book about feelings, discuss the different ways writers show their feelings in their writing. (See Show, Don't Tell, page 38.)

DEMONSTRATION: Reread, revise, and continue your piece of writing, or start a new piece. Find a place to model how writers show feelings in their work. You might say something like, "When this happened I was happy, but instead of writing 'I was happy,' I will write, 'I had a big smile on my face.'"

INVITATION: "Authors, sharing specific details and showing feelings in your writing will help your readers understand what is going on in both your head and your heart. Remember that as you write today!"

MINI-LESSON: WE ALL HAVE OUR OWN UNIQUE VOICE 💬

PREPARATION: Read and discuss either of these books.

The Big Orange Splot (Pinkwater, 1977). Much to his neighbors' chagrin, Mr. Plumbean decides to paint and decorate his house his own way. This "old favorite" story demonstrates the importance of individuality and creativity.

Mr. Tanen's Ties (Cocca-Leffler, 1999). Principal Tanen loves to wear unusual ties, but Mr. Crab Apple does not think it is appropriate. Fortunately, Mr. Apple sees the value of individuality when he receives his own unique tie!

EXPLANATION: This lesson explores the concept of voice as individuality. The concrete, visual examples in either book encourage students to let their own personality shine through their words and illustrations.

DEMONSTRATION: Say, "Today I'm going to take a break from my piece and draw my own [house or tie.]" As you are drawing, comment on your reasoning behind the details you choose to include. Once your illustration is complete, add words to explain why you drew it the way you did.

INVITATION: "Authors, today we're going to do some teacher-guided writing. You are going to create your own 'Mr. Plumbean House' or 'Mr. Tanen Tie.'" Share or display students' diverse works of art and celebrate the different voices of the children in your classroom.

MINI-LESSON: PEOPLE, PLACES, THINGS, AND ANIMALS = NOUNS 📞

PREPARATION:

- Gather a collection of alphabet books or concept books that are brimming with nouns. Here are two of our favorites.

  A Mink, a Fink, a Skating Rink: What Is a Noun? (Cleary, 1999). One of Cleary's many popular books about the parts of speech.

  If You Were a Noun (Dahl, 2006). Also part of a series of colorful books about the parts of speech.

- Prior to reading a noun concept book or alphabet book, write a selection of nouns on cards for the pocket chart. Make sure you have an assortment of people, places, things, and animals to allow students to categorize them.

EXPLANATION: We want children to discover that there are words called nouns that are categorized into people, places, things, and animals.

DEMONSTRATION: After reading the book, gather a collection of words to sort into categories.

INVITATION: "Authors, I'll bet when you reread your work today, you will notice a lot of nouns. When we share, you can show your partner some of your favorite nouns."

MINI-LESSON: TAP YOUR TOES AND STAMP YOUR FEET— LISTEN TO THE AUTHOR'S BEAT

PREPARATION: Select a familiar song or book with an identifiable rhythm.

EXPLANATION: When it comes to sentence fluency, our role as primary grade teachers is to fill children's ears with the sounds of language. Many activities we employ to help strengthen reading fluency, such as choral reading, echo reading, and Readers Theater, are equally beneficial for acquiring an ear for fluent sentence patterns.

DEMONSTRATION: Begin this lesson by humming a familiar song or the rhythm of the words in a book such as Bill Martin Jr.'s *Brown Bear, Brown Bear, What Do You See?* Query students to see if they recognize the song or rhythm you are humming. We've done this lesson with our students for years, and someone always recognizes Martin's distinctive rhythm. Discuss the reasons why it is so easy to recognize, even without hearing the words.

INVITATION: The way that writers listen for fluency is to read their words aloud. "Today before sharing time, I'm going to give you a special signal, and when I give you that signal, I want all of you to read aloud what you've written at the same time." The children enjoy this because it is noisy, but it gets the point across. Continue to stress the importance of rereading work orally throughout the year.

WRITING WORKSHOP TIP:
Partner Sharing Mini-Lesson

"Today we are going to share our writing work with a partner. Let's see what this will look like and sound like." Invite a student to join you as you model the following partner sharing guidelines:

- Sit "eye-to-eye and knee-to-knee" (Miller, 2002).
- Decide who will read first and who will listen.
- If you are the reader, pick a favorite part. Read it slowly, clearly, and loudly.
- If you are the listener, look at your partner. Concentrate and be an active listener.
- After the reader is finished, have a conversation about something you enjoyed about his or her piece and/or ask something you are wondering.
- Switch.
- If you finish before partner sharing time is over, discuss ideas for your next piece of writing.

MINI-LESSON: WORD SWAP ✳

PREPARATION: Locate the following items:

- Your favorite big book. You can use the idea with any big book you are currently reading with your class. For this example we'll use *The Chick and the Duckling* (Ginsburg, 1972).
- Ten small sticky notes to cover one word
- A thesaurus

EXPLANATION: This lesson, adapted from Linda Hoyt's book *Snapshots* (2000, p. 238), helps young writers develop an awareness of words and learn how to make appropriate word choices.

DEMONSTRATION: Place ten small sticky notes over a verb in the book. For example, in *The Chick and the Duckling,* cover the word *cried* in the sentence "'Me too!' cried the Chick." Tell students that you are going to work together and use the thesaurus to think of other words that make sense in that sentence. Some words might include *whimpered, shouted, screamed, shrieked, wailed, sobbed, howled, bawled, screeched, bellowed,* and so on. Write a single verb on each sticky note. Next, arrange the words in order of intensity from quiet to loud. Finally, decide whether the sentence needs a quiet word or a loud word and select the word that best matches the context of the sentence and the illustration.

INVITATION: "Today I'm going to give you some small sticky notes so you can practice this during writing workshop. Cover a word in your own writing and see if you can come up with a better word!"

MINI-LESSON: WHY ARE CONVENTIONS IMPORTANT TO MY READER? ⁉

PREPARATION: Read and discuss *Punctuation Takes a Vacation* (Pulver, 2003). Mr. Wright's students discover how difficult it is to write without punctuation marks.

EXPLANATION: In her book *Creating Young Writers* (2008), Vicki Spandel suggests introducing the concept of conventions by discussing conventions, such as table manners, sportsmanship, and rules of the road, in other areas of our lives. For instance, ask students what the conventions (or rules that we all follow) are in the classroom. They may point out that they use inside voices, listen to each other, take turns, and so on. Next, ask why conventions such as these were created (to make things run smoothly, to make it easier to learn). Liken conventions in school to conventions in writing to emphasize their importance.

DEMONSTRATION: To demonstrate the importance of conventions, write a short piece without any conventions (words upside-down, backwards, starting from the bottom, and so on) and say, "What if conventions took a vacation? Could you read this? Why not?"

INVITATION: "Authors know how important conventions are for their readers. As you reread today, check if you are using conventions to make it easier for your reader."

Part 3: Genre Exploration: Telling Our Story— Personal Narrative

EXPLANATION

You've spent the past two or three weeks setting the stage, building on students' ability to use their words for writing, and introducing students to the inner workings of being an author, the traits of writing, and some basic grammar lessons. Each day you watch children as they slowly begin to fall into the routine: mini-lesson, time for writing, sharing. Up to now, students have been mainly writing and drawing about topics of their own choosing. Some have filled their pages with dinosaur drawings while others have penned clever tales of family adventures, and a few still need a gentle nudge each time they hold their pencils. But you can feel the difference in the workshop already—a routine is starting to take hold. At this point, we would like to switch from the student-choice portion of the workshop to the teacher-guided portion. This is not to say that children's needs and interests will take a back seat, but that we will provide them choice within structure. We will teach them how to write a personal narrative in a developmentally appropriate way, while at the same time encouraging them to choose aspects of their lives they want to share.

PLANNING A GENRE EXPLORATION DAY BY DAY

Here we provide a suggested plan for organizing your genre exploration day by day. Most of the genre explorations contained in this book will take approximately one to two weeks to complete.

Mini-Lessons 1 and 2: Reading Mentor Texts, Planning, and Rehearsing Orally

- Read books to explore the genre. (See chart on page 51.)
- Discuss the characteristics that are specific to this genre; chart the findings.
- Demonstrate how you plan or brainstorm ideas to get started.

- Provide time for students to plan. We've included some planning sheets in the appendices on pages 179–182 (similar to example at right) if you think your students need this added structure.
- Prior to writing, it is helpful if students have the opportunity to talk through their ideas. To model this experience, once you've planned your piece by jotting some main points, tell your students your piece aloud.
- Divide students into pairs or triads and provide time for them to orally rehearse their pieces.

Mea's Personal Narrative Planning Sheet

Mini-Lesson 3: Begin Drafting

If you are using a planning sheet to help organize your ideas, then it is important as you model to stress how to take the ideas from the planning sheet and turn them into meaningful sentences.

Mini-Lessons 4–6: Reread, Revise, and Draft

Each day as you guide students through a piece of writing, it is essential that you demonstrate rereading your piece and revising on the go. As writers, we don't wait until we finish writing to revise, and neither should your students. Watching you reread and revise each time you write will help your students develop this important writing habit.

Mini-Lessons 7–9: Edit, Polish, or Parent Publish

At this point, you have to decide whether you are going to have students simply polish their pieces by adding details to their illustrations or making a fancy cover—or prepare the pieces to Parent Publish. Begin the latter process by setting expectations for editing. For example, if you have taught your students about capital letters and periods, ask them to edit for those particular conventions. Keep in mind that students can't edit for everything. Be specific, model, and guide them as they learn to hunt for their own errors. Once edited, send each student's piece, along with the note in appendix A3, page 173, to parent volunteers.

Mini-Lesson 10: Celebrate!

See page 30 for ideas on celebrating.

September Genre Exploration Chart Telling Our Story: Personal Narrative		
Kid-Friendly Definition of Genre: A personal narrative is a story about something that happened to you and how you feel about it.		
Characteristics of Genre: • Main character is the writer • Usually written in first person • Describes an event or experience • Contains personal comments and observations		
Mentor Texts		
K	1	2
I Like Me! (Carlson, 1988). A charming pig shows that the greatest friend you can have is yourself.	*Fancy Nancy: Bonjour, Butterfly* (O'Connor, 2008). Nancy's narrative illuminates the characteristics of the genre as she tells the story of missing her friend's butterfly birthday party.	*Anna's Table* (Bunting, 2003). While describing her nature collection, Anna shares the memories that match each item. There are helpful samples of focused pieces of writing in the text.
I Like Myself! (Beaumont, 2004). An energetic girl shares all the things she likes about herself.	*Alexander and the Terrible, Horrible, No Good, Very Bad Day* (Viorst, 1972). A classic narrative about a really bad day.	*Pictures From Our Vacation* (Perkins, 2007). The kids fill a notebook with pictures and memories from their vacation.
Zooming In to Align Instruction Across the Grades		
K—All About Me	**1—Personal Narrative**	**2—A Snapshot of My Life**
• Write/draw about likes, dislikes, favorite things, family, and so on. • If needed, use frame sentences such as: I like to _____. My favorite color is _____.	• Write about a specific event. • Craft a narrative that moves through time. • Include interesting details.	• Choose one specific moment on which to focus. • Elaborate by adding feelings, emotions, and sensory details.

A first grader's personal narrative

Final Thoughts

Whew! You made it through the first month of school. Take a moment to catch your breath and congratulate yourself on that tremendous accomplishment. Then, reflect on all the insights into the world of writing your students have experienced in one short month. As September draws to a close, evaluate your students' writing, talk to them about it, celebrate their successes, and use your observations to direct your planning for the upcoming month.

Chapter 3

October:
Exploring Stories

A Sigh of Relief

Can you feel the difference in your teaching days? Are you breathing a sigh of relief as the routines begin to take hold? Happily for us, the steamy days in our classrooms without air conditioning are finally giving way to crisp weather and, as a result, calmer students. It's time to dig in and really start teaching! Based on the interactions with and observations of your learners, you've had the opportunity to determine which writers need support and gentle encouragement and which students display a seemingly innate talent for writing. This information will be helpful as you continue to guide writers during individual and small-group conferences. In the month of September, you introduced, modeled, and practiced numerous procedures, and for most students the routines are becoming second nature. Of course, there are those who will continue to need accommodations and modifications in order to have a successful year. Certainly, students such as these help us to become better teachers.

So we set our sights on October. What's in store? To review, we've launched the writing workshop and familiarized students with many different aspects of writing, including the writing traits, grammar, an awareness of genre, and the essential connection between reading and writing. Students have had ample time to draw and/or write about topics of their choice. During the genre exploration, each child completed a personal narrative capitalizing on individual experiences as a source for ideas. Now is the time for you to determine what your students need next. Will they benefit from more experience with personal narrative writing? If that is the case, you may want to spend another week or so focused on that particular genre exploration. For many young writers, personal narrative is a comfortable genre they will repeatedly revisit in their "student choice" writing. For that reason, continue to encourage them during conferences to hone their personal narratives, but move on to other aspects of writing during your mini-lessons. With that goal in mind, sample the mini-lessons in this chapter designed to broaden students' writing repertoire. This chapter ends with a genre exploration in which children write stories about themselves or other characters, comprised of either real-life or make-believe happenings, or maybe a little of both!

Part 1: Morning Message Ideas and Samples

After experimenting with the various messages in the September chapter, perhaps you've discovered that your students have some favorites. Do they enjoy it when the "letter stealer" swipes key letters? On the other hand, you may have noticed that certain messages (such as Where Do the Periods Go?) require repetition. We are hopeful that you have started creating your own messages based on your particular curriculum and students. As we add to your collection, don't forget to revisit messages from previous chapters to strengthen areas of need in your students' writing.

MORNING MESSAGE IDEA: OCTOBER WORD CHART

See explanation on page 35.

> ### Morning Message Sample
>
> #### October Word Chart
>
> | | | |
> |---|---|---|
> | Columbus Day | Halloween | pumpkin |
> | trick-or-treat | costume | candy |
> | leaves | party | jack-o'-lantern |
> | decorations | apple-picking | fall |

MORNING MESSAGE IDEA: USING RIDDLES TO TEACH THE CONCEPT OF A SENTENCE

Simply put, kids love writing riddles. In fact, once you introduce riddles to your young writers, they may go a little "riddle crazy." Consequently, riddles will frequently appear in their journals. We utilize riddles because they provide another means to teach the concept of a sentence. When you stress that each clue is a sentence, it provides a concrete way to explain the use of beginning capital letters and ending marks. You can also use riddles to review topics covered in your science and social studies curriculum. It is important to point out that we strive to make each morning message as interactive as possible, with a number of students joining us each day to add words, punctuation, and so on. Don't wait for one child to sit down before another comes up, but instead show the children how to pass the chalk or marker to one another while you continue making teaching points. To sustain students' interest as others are writing, engage in an ongoing dialogue about the process. To give you an idea of what this might sound like, we've recorded our conversation as we introduce riddle writing to our kids.

Sam's riddle

T: Let's write a riddle about a pumpkin. Turn and tell your neighbor what you know about pumpkins.
[Give students a minute to talk with and listen to their neighbor.]

T: Can anyone tell me a clue about a pumpkin?

S: It is orange.

For kindergarten or first-grade students you might say,

T: That's a helpful clue. How many words is that? Show me with your fingers. [This is always interesting!]

T: Listen carefully; do you hear three words? Let me draw a line for each word.
[Draw three lines on the chalkboard or chart paper.]

T: Can someone walk up to the chalkboard and write the word *it*? What kind of letter does *it* need at the beginning?

S: A capital letter.

T: Smart thinking! Why does it need a capital letter?

S: Because it is at the beginning.

T: Yes! Writers put a capital letter at the beginning of a clue because each clue is a sentence.

T: Oh look, the word *is* is on the word wall. Glance at the word wall as you're writing if you're not sure how to spell it.

T: Finally, let's write the word *orange*. Can you find the word *orange* somewhere in our room?

S: It's on the poster hanging near the door.

T: Good detective work! The color word *orange* is on the poster hanging right there on the wall; whenever you need to spell a color word, you can look right here! [Walk over to the poster and point to it.]

Continue the process as you write two more clues, the question, and the answer.

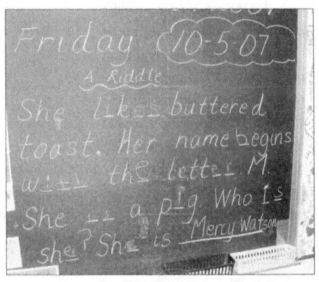

Morning Message Sample

Using Riddles to Teach the Concept of a Sentence

It is hot. It is a star. It is at the center of our solar system. What is it? It is the _____.

A sampling of morning message riddles

MORNING MESSAGE IDEA: WHAT KIND OF SENTENCE, TELLING OR ASKING?

Each time we pose the query "Do you have any questions?" we are reminded how difficult it is for young learners to discriminate between "telling" and "asking" sentences. Indeed, this is equally apparent in their writing. To begin an ongoing dialogue about the appropriate ending punctuation for each type of sentence, try this message. Before students arrive, write each sentence without the ending punctuation. To keep the message brief, work with only three or four sentences each day. We've provided enough sentences in our sample for a few days worth of messages.

MORNING MESSAGE IDEA: DISCOVERING DETAILS

We suggest using this message as a follow-up to The Details of Your Day mini-lesson found on page 67. Young children constantly remind us how important it is to explicitly teach and model the skills and concepts in our curriculum. We're sure you have had the experience of quickly teaching a lesson and running out of time to clearly explain and model. Then, when you invite students to try it out on their own, you discover that the students are unsure what to do, their hands waving wildly as you realize your mistake. After a lesson like this, we toss the papers in our neighbor's recycling bin (so the kids don't see them) and begin again the

---

Morning Message Sample

What Kind of Sentence, Telling or Asking?

Is this sentence a "telling" sentence or an "asking" sentence?

Columbus sailed three ships (.)

Who was Christopher Columbus (?)

People thought the world was flat (.)

When did Columbus sail (?)

Columbus used the stars to guide his way (.)

Where was Columbus trying to sail (?)

Columbus was an explorer (.)

What did Columbus call the Native Americans (?)

Columbus Day is on Monday (.)

The leaves are changing colors (.)

Why do the leaves change colors (?)

The days are getting shorter (.)

What time does it get dark (?)

The birds begin to fly south (.)

Why do some birds fly in a "V" shape (?)

Pumpkins grow on a vine (.)

Where did you find that huge pumpkin (?)

It is chilly outside today (.)

Did you wear a jacket (?)

next day! Well, the same can be said for the concept of details. We often ask children to add details to their illustrations and stories but don't always take the time to show them how to do it. This message is ideal for demonstrating how to add details.

Begin by writing a "sketchy story" about a recent event in your life. Choose a personal experience such as a family outing or a memorable occasion.

Next, explain to the students that one way to add details to a piece of writing is to anticipate the reader's questions in order to elaborate on the events being described. To assist you in this task, invite students to ask you questions about your sketchy story. To help students differentiate among questions, consider writing each question in a different color. Maria's first graders generated the questions at right in response to her Arboretum story.

This is a good stopping place for young learners. The next day, rewrite your sketchy story in front of students by attempting to answer each question. If this book were printed in color, you would see that we write the answers in the color that matches the question.

Morning Message Sample

Discovering Details

We went to the Arboretum.
We walked around.
We had fun.

What did you do there?
What did you see there?
What was your favorite part?
Who did you go with?
When did you go there?
Where is the Arboretum?
How did you get there?
Why was it fun?

My Revised Piece

On Sunday morning, Mr. Walther, Alyona, Katie, and I drove our van to Lisle, Illinois, to visit the Arboretum. We saw a 1,000-pound pumpkin, scarecrows decorated by Brownie troops, and a castle made of branches. We hiked, ate caramel apples, and watched an expert pumpkin carver. My favorite part was watching Katie and Alyona run and play. It was an enjoyable family morning because we were together.

A Sketchy Story

I went to the apple orchard.
We bought caramel apples and donuts.
It was fun.

Who? Who did you go with?
What? What did you do there?
Where? Where was the orchard?
When? When did you go?
Why? Why did you go?

A Super Story!

Last Saturday I went to the apple orchard with my friend Kim. We drove to Maple Park, IL. to see the trees and pumpkins. We wanted to have some fall fun! We shopped for apples, donuts, caramel apples, pumpkins and indian corn. We walked around the farm and had a fabulous time!

Ms. Phillips's Discovering Details chart

MORNING MESSAGE IDEA: WORD EXCHANGE

See explanation on page 37.

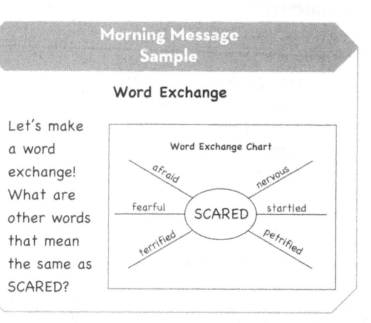

Morning Message Sample

Word Exchange

Let's make a word exchange! What are other words that mean the same as SCARED?

Word Exchange Chart

afraid nervous
fearful SCARED startled
terrified petrified

MORNING MESSAGE IDEA: THE LETTER STEALER—SHORT VOWELS

See explanation on page 39.

Morning Message Sample

The Letter Stealer—Short Vowels

A bl_ck c_t w_ll j_mp _p _n the r_d br_ck wall.
(A black cat will jump up on the red brick wall.)

MORNING MESSAGE IDEA: WHAT IS THIS SENTENCE MISSING?

To raise students' awareness of the necessity of verbs in sentences, write sentences in which the verb is missing. Begin by asking students if they notice anything wrong with the "sentences," then continue by inviting students to supply a number of possible verbs that could complete each sentence.

> ### Morning Message Sample
>
> **What Is This Sentence Missing?**
>
> Sarah in the pool (possible responses: jumped, splashed, frolicked)
> The children to school (possible responses: skipped, rode, strolled, ran)
> A boy the ball (possible responses: caught, tossed, pitched, lobbed, whacked)

MORNING MESSAGE IDEA: WHOSE VOICE DO YOU HEAR?

One element of voice is that it enables the reader to learn about the character through his or her words. Use this light-hearted message to demonstrate how writers can illuminate a character by writing with a distinctive voice in mind.

> ### Morning Message Sample
>
> **Whose Voice Do You Hear?**
>
> I vant to vish you a Happy Halloveen! (vampire)
> The schooooooool looooooooks coooooool on this spooooooky day. (ghost)
> Whooooooo is sitting in my tree? (owl)
> Yum! There is a delicious bug stuck in my delicate home. (spider)
> Eeeeeeeeek! I'm hanging by my feet. (bat)

MORNING MESSAGE IDEA: THESAURUS THURSDAY

One way to incorporate word choice messages into your weekly routine is by designating a special day to use the thesaurus to discover new and interesting words. In this sample, the students created a list of spooky sounds after listening to a spooky sounds recording.

Read-Alouds for Writers		
Title and Author	**Brief Summary**	**Focus**
If I Built a Car (Van Dusen, 2005)	Jack describes every detail of his spectacular fantasy car. Pair this with the poem "Michael Built a Bicycle" from *The New Kid on the Block* (Prelutsky, 1984).	Ideas: Details
It Begins With an A (Calmenson, 1993)	Use this alphabet book to reinforce the concept of riddles.	Ideas/Organization: Riddles
The Little Old Lady Who Was Not Afraid of Anything (Williams, 1986)	This book is perfect for choral reading or Readers Theater. The students enjoy joining in as the animated objects try to scare the little old lady.	Word Choice: Onomatopoeia Organization: Cumulative Tale
Mercy Watson: Princess in Disguise (DiCamillo, 2007)	DiCamillo has created a memorable, humorous character in Mercy the pig. In this book, the Watsons dress her up and take her trick-or-treating.	Ideas: Character
Nouns and Verbs Have a Field Day (Pulver, 2006)	The nouns and verbs enjoy a field day of their own after the class goes out to play.	Grammar
Rattlebone Rock (Andrews, 1995)	Highlight sentence fluency with this rollicking, rhythmic Halloween tale.	Sentence Fluency
Room on the Broom (Donaldson, 2001)	A friendly witch invites some helpful animals to join her for a spin on her broom. A bouncy rhyming tale!	Sentence Fluency
Shake Dem Halloween Bones (Nikola-Lisa, 1997)	The kids will tap their toes as you read this October favorite.	Sentence Fluency
The Vowel Family: A Tale of Lost Letters (Walker, 2008)	Don't miss this creative, humorous story that clearly demonstrates the importance of vowels.	Conventions: Vowels
Woolbur (Helakoski, 2008)	Free-spirited Woolbur doesn't want to act like every other sheep in the flock.	Voice

Part 2: A Menu of Mini-Lessons—Celebrating the Story

One of the favorite times of our teaching day is when we gather our students around us to read aloud. Undoubtedly, you've already shared some of your favorite stories with your class. This year some of our students couldn't get enough of the humorous circular story *When a Monster Is Born* (Taylor, 2006), while others preferred Jack the farm cat's tale of *The Perfect Nest* (Friend, 2007). What is it about well-written stories that prompt the joyful chorus of "Read it again!"? Talented writers create a mood and fill their stories with action that spurs us to keep reading. Their stories have engaging beginnings, detailed middles, and satisfying conclusions. Obviously, many of the stories we read aloud are far more elaborate than those our students are currently writing, but we keep reading because our job as primary grade teachers is to fill our children with the language of story.

Catherine Friend   illustrated by John Manders

Store students' finished pieces in a writing portfolio.

WRITING WORKSHOP TIP:
Where Will Finished Pieces Be Stored?

One option for storing students' polished or published work is a writing portfolio. This portfolio is not an assessment portfolio; rather, it is a collection of the author's finished work. Similar to an artist's portfolio, students will enjoy sharing their polished pieces with their peers, cross-age buddies, and, of course, their parents at the end of the year.

MINI-LESSON: LOOKING FOR IDEAS? REACH FOR A WORDLESS PICTURE BOOK 🔦

PREPARATION:

- Choose a wordless picture book from the chart below to share with students. If possible, make overheads of a few key illustrations or share the book using a document camera.
- Gather wordless picture books to keep handy in your writing center.

EXPLANATION: Wordless books are a useful resource to help reluctant writers spark story ideas.

DEMONSTRATION: "Sometimes when I can't think of any ideas for writing, I pick up a wordless picture book. Let's take a look through this book and tell the story together as we turn the pages." As you take a picture walk through the text, invite different students to tell the story of each picture. Discuss how they could use these stories as seed ideas for their own writing. Model writing a short piece based on one of the ideas you discussed.

INVITATION: "Writers, if you are ever stuck and can't think of an idea, this basket of books will be available to help spark your imagination."

Looking for Ideas? Reach for a Wordless Picture Book.	
Title and Author	**Brief Summary**
Bow-Wow Bugs a Bug (Newgarden & Cash, 2007)	Bow-Wow follows a black bug around town.
Deep in the Forest (Turkle, 1976)	A wordless account of the Goldilocks tale
The Last Laugh (Aruego, 2006)	A bullying snake is outwitted by a clever duck.
Museum Trip (Lehman, 2006)	A boy on a field trip imagines himself inside the museum exhibits.
Peep! (Luthardt, 2003)	A boy befriends a yellow duckling.
Rainstorm (Lehman, 2007)	A mysterious key opens a large trunk with a ladder inside—and a child finds friends and fun.
Un-brella (Franson, 2007)	A girl's magical umbrella helps to brighten a gray winter day.
Wave (Lee, 2008) 	Enjoy a day at the beach with an energetic young girl.

MINI-LESSON: WORKING WITH WORD FAMILIES— A USEFUL SPELLING STRATEGY

PREPARATION: Select a rime that will help children spell a large number of words. According to Edward Fry (1998), the following rimes are the most common based on frequency. For a complete list, see Fry's article "Teaching Reading: The Most Common Phonograms" in *The Reading Teacher*.

-ay (26 words)	-ill (26 words)	-ip (22 words)	-at (19 words)
-am (19 words)	-ag (19 words)	-ack (19 words)	-ank (19 words)
-ick (19 words)	-ell (18 words)	-ot (18 words)	-ing (18 words)

EXPLANATION: This mini-lesson reinforces the concept that knowing word families is a useful spelling strategy. This strategy is helpful in both writing and reading.

DEMONSTRATION: Begin with an explanation such as, "Today before I continue my writing, I want to think about what writers do when they have to spell the word *day*. I'm going to think of other words I know that are spelled the same way as *day*. Can you help me make a list? If you can spell *day*, what else can you spell?" Record the words on a chart and display for reference, or encourage students to make their own list in their writer's notebook.

INVITATION: "Authors, today while you are writing, look for words that are spelled like other words you know. That's what writers do."

MINI-LESSON: INTRODUCING VERBS

PREPARATION: Read and discuss one of these books.

Add It, Dip It, Fix It: A Book of Verbs (Schneider, 1995). This book is ideal for kindergartners. It is a simple, alphabetically organized introduction to verbs.

Who Hoots? (Davis, 2000) and *Who Hops?* (Davis, 1998). Both of these entertaining books offer a predictable question-answer format and bright illustrations that make them wonderful read-aloud selections.

EXPLANATION: The purpose of this mini-lesson is to teach students that verbs are action words.

DEMONSTRATION: After reading, write a few verbs from the book on index cards or the chalkboard. From *Who Hops?* choose the words *hops*, *flies*, *slithers*, *swims*, and *crawls*; or from *Who Hoots?*

select *hoots*, *buzzes*, *squeaks*, *roars*, and *quacks*. Ask, "Can anyone tell me how these words are alike?" Next, discuss how the words describe things that animals or people do. Explain that action words such as these are called *verbs*. Finally, brainstorm a list of action words for people. Some may include *talk*, *jump*, *play*, *hide*, *scream*, *sing*, *walk*, *run*, *write*, and *read*. Later, return to these words to brainstorm more colorful alternatives.

INVITATION: "Writers, today I want you to notice how you use verbs to tell about what your characters are doing."

MINI-LESSON: SENTENCE SLEUTHS—NOUNS AND VERBS

PREPARATION: Read and discuss one of these selections: *If You Were a Verb* (Dahl, 2006) or *To Root, To Toot, To Parachute: What Is a Verb?* (Cleary, 2001).

Write the following sentences on sentence strips. Print all the nouns in one color and all the verbs in another color. Cut each strip as indicated, between the noun and the verb.

The dog/barks.
The cat/meows.
The monkey/swings.
The snake/slithers.

The bird/flies.	The mouse/squeaks.
The rabbit/hops.	The owl/hoots.
The fish/swims.	The bear/growls.
The bee/stings.	The worm/wiggles.

EXPLANATION: This mini-lesson is designed to help students identify and distinguish between nouns and verbs.

DEMONSTRATION: Introduce this lesson by saying, "Today we are going to play a game called 'Sentence Sleuths.' Do you know what it means to be a sleuth?" Pass out one sentence part to each student. Remind them that the sentences they write need to have both nouns and verbs. Then, invite students to find the classmate who has the matching part to their sentence. Once they've found that person, the pair should sit down together and quietly read their sentence. Give the learners an opportunity to brainstorm other verbs that would make sense with their noun by supplying them with a few sticky notes to place on top of the verb. To conclude, ask students to share their original sentence and two new verbs. Before students begin writing, continue to demonstrate your own writing. As you model, you may want to choose a verb or two and ask the students to supply some alternatives.

INVITATION: "Authors, as you are writing today notice the nouns and verbs in your sentences. Could you use a different, more vivid verb to say the same thing?"

MINI-LESSON: ADDING ACTION TO YOUR STORY

The sentence sleuths read their sentences on "Wear Your Sunglasses Day."

PREPARATION: Read and discuss *Move!* (Jenkins & Page, 2006), in which the authors describe all the different ways animals move.

EXPLANATION: Vivid verbs give writing a boost. Jenkins and Page's book offers writers a collection of words that describe how animals move.

DEMONSTRATION: "Let's record all of the verbs Steve Jenkins uses in his book. Can you add to our collection?"

INVITATION: "While you are writing today, notice that a slight change in the verbs you choose can make your character's actions more vivid."

A collection of verbs based on *Move!*

MINI-LESSON: THE BUILDING BLOCKS OF ORGANIZATION

PREPARATION:

- Copy the building block graphic organizer found in Appendix A8 on page 180. You may choose to cut apart the blocks so you can give the group three separate blocks.

- Divide students into groups of three.
- Give building blocks to each group of students.

EXPLANATION: This lesson provides students with an opportunity to learn from one another as they team up to create a story.

DEMONSTRATION:

1. Begin this lesson by modeling your own simple story on the building blocks.
2. Give each triad their building blocks.
3. Before doing any writing, each group must agree on a topic and then decide who is going to write the beginning, middle, and end. When they have completed this task, they should raise their hands and orally share their story with you.
4. Students write and illustrate their specific part of the story.
5. If you choose, students can glue their completed building blocks on a 12" x 18" sheet of construction paper to display on a bulletin board.

INVITATION: "Writers, today you worked with a group to create a story. As you work on your own, remember how helpful it is to talk with others about your ideas for writing."

MINI-LESSON: THE DETAILS OF YOUR DAY

PREPARATION: You may choose to read a story about school such as *Never Spit on Your Shoes* (Cazet, 1990).

EXPLANATION: How often have you handed a paper back to a child and said, "Please add details"? I'm sure we've all done this numerous times. The missing piece in this writing instruction is actually showing children exactly what we mean by the words "add details."

DEMONSTRATION: To demonstrate this, we begin with a scenario that is very familiar to students. Tell them, "Today during writing workshop we are going to talk about details. Does anyone know what details are?" Listen to and discuss responses. Continue, "When you go home from school, I bet your family asks, 'What did you do at school today?' How do you answer?" Record student responses. Prompt by saying, "Now let's look at how we can add details to your answers."

Original Answer	Detailed Answer
I ate lunch.	I had cheese pizza for lunch.
We read a book.	Ms. Phillips read the first chapter of *Judy Moody*.
We had recess.	I played tag with Ali and Eric on the playground.

INVITATION: "As a writer, it is important that you add details in your piece, just like we did today during our mini-lesson."

MINI-LESSON: LET'S COLLECT WORDS, PART 1 ✦

PREPARATION:

- Make enough copies of the family letter found below so you have one for each student, and staple each note to a lunch bag. You will send these home with students.

- Cut a few words out of a magazine or newspaper and place them in your own bag for the demonstration lesson.

- Read and discuss *Max's Words* (Banks, 2006), in which Max collects, sorts, and organizes his word collection to create thoughts and stories.

EXPLANATION: Young writers tend to choose the same words over and over again. Sometimes this is because they are easy to encode and write; other times it is simply due to a lack of exposure to a variety of words. This lesson is designed to motivate children to seek out alternative word choices as they are writing.

DEMONSTRATION: Say, "Wow! Max did a lot of interesting things with his words. Tonight when you go home, you are going to begin a word collection of your very own. First, let's think about what makes a word interesting and jot down some ideas on our chart. Let's look through this magazine to see if we can find some words to add to the collection that I have already started in this bag." Reach in and pull out a few words. Explain why you chose those words and why they are interesting to you. "Today I'm going to try to use these words as I write." Write a short piece using the words you found in your bag.

INVITATION: "When you are writing today, take a careful look at your words. Are you using the same words over and over again? Could you swap a word for a better word?"

Let's Collect Words Family Letter

Dear Families,

Today during writing workshop we read a story called *Max's Words*. In the book, Max collected words from magazines, newspapers, and other printed materials around his house. Please help your child find and cut out or write five to ten interesting words. Try to select words that are in large-size print! Please return your child's word collection by

_____.

Thanks for your continued support!
Your Child's Teacher

MINI-LESSON: LET'S COLLECT WORDS, PART 2

DEMONSTRATION: Say, "I'm going to reach into my word collection again to see what I find." Write another short piece using the words you found in your bag or discuss different ways the words could be used in writing.

INVITATION: "Authors, now it's your turn. During writing time today, I would like you to meet with a group of your classmates. Reach into your word collection, pull out a word or two, and share the words with your group. Discuss how you might use each word in your writing, to describe characters, setting, and so on. When you are finished, you may begin writing. See if you can revise a previous piece by exchanging an old word for a new, more interesting word."

MINI-LESSON: THE WHO AND WHY OF WRITING 🗩

PREPARATION: Collect three different types of texts. Some possibilities include restaurant menus, picture books, travel brochures, joke or riddle books, poems, advertisements, game directions, comic strips, and songs.

EXPLANATION: This lesson uses everyday texts to help introduce the concept of audience and purpose.

DEMONSTRATION: Say to students, "Let's take a look at these three different types of texts. Let's try to figure out for whom the author was writing the text and why the author wrote it. The 'who' and 'why' of writing have names. The 'who' is called the audience and the 'why' is called the purpose." To record students' thinking, make a chart detailing the audience and purpose for each type of writing.

INVITATION: "Authors, as you are writing, think about your audience and purpose."

MINI-LESSON: DETAILS ADD VOICE TO YOUR ILLUSTRATIONS 🗩

PREPARATION: Create a poster similar to the one pictured at right.

EXPLANATION: Dedicating a mini-lesson or two to discussing and teaching children how to create detailed illustrations will pay off as the year progresses. We find it helpful to review this mini-lesson after the break in January and again in the spring.

DEMONSTRATION: Discuss each illustration, beginning with the plain stick figure. Pose some of the following questions: "What can you tell me about this illustration? Can you tell if it is a boy or girl? Do you know where this character is and what he or she is doing? What details in the illustration help you answer these questions?" Continue to look through the pictures and see if you can begin to answer the questions.

INVITATION: "Artists, as you create your illustrations, think about how you can add voice to your drawings simply by adding creative details."

MINI-LESSON: SEARCHING FOR SENTENCE FLUENCY

PREPARATION: Read aloud books with distinctive sentence fluency. See Read-Alouds for Writers on page 61 for some suggestions.

EXPLANATION: Young writers need to hear numerous examples of fluent writing. As you read aloud books in which writers have used various techniques, point them out.

DEMONSTRATION: After reading a book with rhythm and rhyme ask, "What did you notice as I read that book?" Discuss the author's use of rhythm, rhyme, and other elements.

INVITATION: "Authors, remember the best way to hear fluency in your writing is by reading your work aloud. I'll remind you before we share to take a moment to read your work aloud to yourself."

MINI-LESSON: QUESTION MARKS

PREPARATION: Read and discuss books that use question words. Below are some examples.

What Do You Do With a Tail Like This? (Jenkins & Page, 2003). Discover how animals use their noses, ears, tails, eyes, mouths, and feet.

Where Are You Going, Little Mouse? (Kraus, 1986). In the sequel to *Whose Mouse Are You?*, Little Mouse runs away from home.

Why Did the Chicken Cross the Road? (Frazee et al., 2006). Fourteen illustrators offer their answers to the classic joke. If your students enjoy this book, look for *Knock, Knock!* (Freyman et al., 2007).

EXPLANATION: This lesson is helpful in introducing students to different words that signal a question.

DEMONSTRATION: Ask students, "Can you name a word that signals a question?" Make a list of "question words." Using the question words on the list, ask students to turn and talk with a partner about a question they could ask, and then answer in writing. Model by writing a short piece beginning with a question such as "Where are you going, Mr. Bear?"

INVITATION: "Writers, if you choose, you can write or illustrate your own answers to the question, such as 'Why did the chicken cross the road?' or 'What do you do with a ___ like this?'"

Part 3: Genre Exploration: Writing a Story— The Basics

EXPLANATION

For this month's teacher-guided genre exploration, students will use the knowledge they gained from the morning messages and mini-lessons to create their own story, with the focus on including a beginning, a middle, and an end. We've provided two different planning sheets in Appendix A8 (page 180) and Appendix A9 (page 181) to match the varying abilities of your writers. For additional hints about day-by-day planning, return to pages 49–50.

October Genre Exploration Chart Writing a Story: The Basics		
Kid-Friendly Definition of Genre: A story is when you tell someone about something that has happened. It can be real or make-believe.		
Characteristics of Genre: • Main character can be the writer or another person or creature. • Author uses his or her imagination to create the tale. • Written in either first person or third person. • Narrates a chain of related events. • Contains a beginning, a middle, and an end.		
Mentor Texts		
K	**1**	**2**
Bad Dog, Marley! (Grogan, 2007). Marley joins the family. Marley gets into a lot of trouble. Finally, Marley saves the day. This is an ideal example of a humorous text with a clear beginning, middle, and end.	*Miss Malarkey Doesn't Live in Room 10* (Finchler, 1995). A young boy narrates this funny and realistic story about his teacher. *The Wolf's Chicken Stew* (Kasza, 1987). This is an imaginative tale about a hungry wolf.	*Once Upon a Cool Motorcycle Dude* (O'Malley, 2005). A boy and a girl each tell their version of a fairy tale. Don't miss this humorous and voice-filled book. *The Paper Bag Princess* (Munsch, 1980). Princess Elizabeth rescues an ungrateful prince.
Zooming In to Align Instruction Across the Grades		
K—Simple Stories	**1—Eventful Fiction**	**2—Fabulous Fantasy**
• Students write/draw real stories. • Focus on the three main parts.	• Students write either real or make-believe stories. • Encourage and expect students to add more events in the middle.	• Students write make-believe stories. • Encourage and expect students to add more detailed events in the middle.

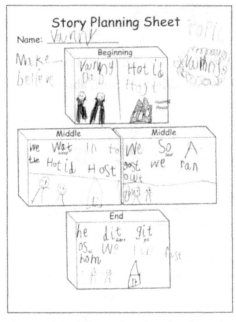

A completed story planning sheet—and the resulting story (in the following thumbnails)

One night, Vanny and his dad ate dinner. They took the trash out. They saw a haunted house. We went to it. We heard a noise.

We knocked on the door. Nobody was there. I knocked again. Nobody was there. We just went right in. It was dark. We saw a haunted stairs.

Final Thoughts

The excitement builds as students become more adept at composing and creating memorable stories that incorporate the many writers' techniques that you've shared this month. You may notice that one child used a vivid verb in his story, while another student spent time studying a wordless book when searching for an idea. Moments like these remind us of the essential role children's literature plays in the teaching of writing, of our responsibility to fill children with the language of story, and of the endless possibilities students have as writers of their own stories.

We didn't go upstairs. We checked around. Everything was dark. We just went upstairs. We saw a little light. We went to the light. Something popped out.

We were scared. It was dark. We ran down the stairs. Then another thing popped out. We crawled under his legs. We ran home!

Chapter 4

November & December: Zooming In on Story Elements

Two Busy Months

How can it possibly be November? It seems as if we just began, and then, in the blink of an eye, we are one quarter of the way through the school year. For many of us, November is a short month packed to the brim with report cards, parent-teacher conferences, and a few days off for the Thanksgiving holiday (hooray!). Before long, the calendar flips over to the month of December, another eventful time in elementary school. It is clear why we chose to combine these two hectic months into one chapter. This chapter will expand on the story basics introduced last month by focusing on the story elements, including characters, setting, events, problem, and solution. Also, you will build on students' grammar knowledge of nouns and verbs by introducing and exploring adjectives.

Part 1: Morning Message Ideas and Samples

By now we hope we've convinced you that the morning message is an essential part of your teaching day. It is amazing how many concepts you can teach and review in the morning message day after day. Moreover, students come to depend on the message as a time for you to set the stage for the day, teach and review writing strategies, and preview upcoming special events. As you can see in the photograph at right, we post our daily schedule next to the message and review it after completing the message. This is a helpful visual cue, especially for students who struggle with transitions and changes in routine. For November and December, the messages are a bit more complex and will require repetition over a few days to increase students' expertise.

Post your daily schedule near your message for an overview of the day's events.

MORNING MESSAGE IDEA: NOVEMBER AND DECEMBER WORD CHARTS

See explanation on page 35.

> **Morning Message Sample**
>
> ### November Word Chart
>
> | | | |
> |---|---|---|
> | Thanksgiving | turkey | football |
> | pie | conferences | pilgrims |
> | grandma | grandpa | house |
> | feast | dinner | Native Americans |

> **Morning Message Sample**
>
> ### December Word Chart
>
> | | |
> |---|---|
> | tree | shopping |
> | snow | candles |
> | family | decorate |
> | holiday | presents |
> | celebrate | cookies |
> | party | cocoa |

MORNING MESSAGE IDEA: COMPARING CHARACTERS

During read-aloud time, you have already shared many books with memorable characters. For this message, choose two similar characters and, using a Venn diagram or H-chart, guide students as they compare the characters. Ask, "How are the two characters alike and how are they different?"

Some characters that work well for this message:

Olivia, Mercy Watson, Poppleton
    (all pigs, make-believe)

Mudge, Clifford, Marley (all dogs, some
    realistic, others make-believe)

Judy Moody, Junie B. Jones, Clementine
    (all females, realistic)

Cam Jansen, Jigsaw Jones, Nate the Great
    (all detectives, realistic)

Franklin, Froggy, Arthur (all animals,
    make-believe)

MORNING MESSAGE IDEA: THE MYSTERY CHARACTER 🔊

The mystery character message uses riddles, introduced in the October chapter, to highlight character traits. To add suspense, reveal one clue at a time. Begin with a broad clue and then continue with more specific ones. Once students are familiar with the mystery character format, work in a shared writing mode to create riddles together.

Morning Message Sample

Comparing characters using an H-chart

A mystery character riddle about Jigsaw Jones

Morning Message Sample

The Mystery Character

The mystery character is a pig. The mystery character has neighbors. The mystery character loves buttered toast. Who is the mystery character? (Mercy Watson)	The mystery character is a dog. The mystery character is huge. The mystery character lives with Henry. Who is the mystery character? (Mudge)
The mystery character is a bird. The mystery character is odd. The mystery character lives on an iceberg. Who is the mystery character? (Tacky)	The mystery character is a boy. The mystery character creates comic strips. The mystery character has a sister named Judy Moody. Who is the mystery character? (Stink)

MORNING MESSAGE IDEA: SETTINGS AND SENSES

This Setting and Senses message works well as a follow-up to the mini-lesson found on page 83. To launch this message, review the five senses or read Shelley Rotner's book *Senses in the City* (2008). Then, explain how writers use their senses to help them describe the setting of a story. Consider focusing on one or two senses during each message time.

Morning Message Sample

Settings and Senses

Choose a specific setting such as the classroom, the zoo, a stormy night, a castle, the bottom of the ocean, the planet Mars, a farm, or your backyard. Create the chart shown here. Guide students to brainstorm a list of descriptive words and phrases by using the following prompts.

- Close your eyes. What would you see in this setting?
- Listen carefully. What would you hear?
- Would you taste or smell anything?
- If you were standing in this setting, what would you feel? Would you feel a cool breeze, the warm sun, the fur of an animal, or something else?

Today's setting is _____.	
I see	I hear
I taste/smell	I feel

MORNING MESSAGE IDEA: SORTING NOUNS, VERBS, AND ADJECTIVES

This message is an extension of the adjective mini-lesson found on page 82. To prepare, prewrite a list of words and make a chart with the headings Noun, Verb, and Adjective. As you read each word, invite students to write the word under the correct heading. Note that some words will fit into more than one category, which leads to meaningful discussions.

Morning Message Sample

Sorting Nouns, Verbs, and Adjectives

Thanksgiving: eat, turkey, yummy, family, laugh, football, juicy, play, share, flavorful

Fall: leaves, jump, run, chilly, rake, colorful, windy, crunch, scarecrow, cornucopia

Holidays: party, merry, cookies, sing, food, presents, give, sweet, joyful, cook

Winter: snow, jacket, snowman, shiny, sled, build, throw, snowball, ride, chilly

MORNING MESSAGE IDEA: LOOKING FOR IDEAS? TELL US HOW YOU FEEL TODAY

We created this message to aid students still searching for ideas. We simply ask students to write about how they are feeling. To expand writers' vocabularies, brainstorm different word choices for the common feelings children will share, such as happy and sad. On a chart, list students' feelings and the reasons for those particular feelings.

> **Morning Message Sample**
>
> Looking for Ideas? Tell Us How You Feel Today
>
> How do you feel today?
> Feeling   Why?

MORNING MESSAGE IDEA: THE LETTER STEALER—LONG VOWEL/SILENT e

See explanation on page 39.

> **Morning Message Sample**
>
> The Letter Stealer—Long Vowel/Silent e
>
> The c_t_ wh_t_ bear will d_z_ in his c_v_.
> (The cute white bear will doze in his cave.)
> I will _s_ the st_v_ to b_k_ f_v_ h_g_ c_k_s.
> (I will use the stove to bake five huge cakes.)

MORNING MESSAGE IDEA: REREAD YOUR PIECE ALOUD WITH VOICE

How do we encourage students to get into the habit of rereading their written work? One way is to model rereading in the morning message. Each time you and your students complete the work of the message, go back to the beginning and reread. This leads into a conversation about reading with fluency and expression, and listening to the voice of the writer. A book that reinforces this concept is *Wolf!* (Bloom, 1999), about a wolf who learns that reading well means reading with enthusiasm and passion. Launch this message by reading the sentences in a choppy, monotone voice, and then challenge students to read it orally with voice!

> **Morning Message Sample**
>
> Reread Your Piece Aloud With Voice
>
> Good morning, readers and writers! I can't wait to learn something new from you today. Do you know what holiday is coming soon? SMILE and MAKE GOOD CHOICES!

MORNING MESSAGE IDEA: WORD EXCHANGE

See explanation on page 37.

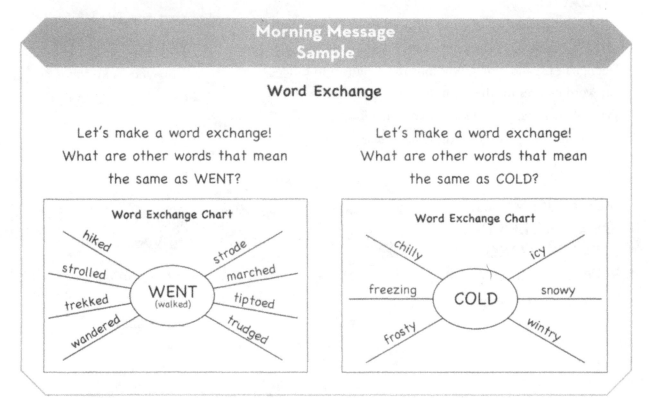

Morning Message Sample

Word Exchange

Let's make a word exchange! What are other words that mean the same as WENT?

Word Exchange Chart

hiked
strolled
trekked
wandered
WENT (walked)
strode
marched
tiptoed
trudged

Let's make a word exchange! What are other words that mean the same as COLD?

Word Exchange Chart

chilly
freezing
frosty
COLD
icy
snowy
wintry

MORNING MESSAGE IDEA: CREATIVE CONVENTIONS

Authors, illustrators, and designers work together to convey meaning through a book's words, and they often employ unique conventions such as wavy writing, words that are bold and capitalized, and words that show movement in different ways. As you enjoy books with your students, point out creative conventions. See the Read-Alouds for Writers chart on page 79 for a few of our favorite titles. Then, highlight various conventions in the morning message. Here are just a few ideas to get you started. We're sure your students will be able to think of many more!

Morning Message Sample

Creative Conventions

How does the author want you to read these words?

WATCH OUT!

The mouse is walking over the hill.

The snowman fell 𝘰𝘰𝘻𝘻.

The ghost said, "BOOOOOO!"

Read-Alouds for Writers

Title and Author	Brief Summary	Focus
I Know an Old Lady Who Swallowed a Pie (Jackson, 1997)	Students will enjoy this humorous Thanksgiving version of a familiar folk song.	Sentence Fluency
I Stink! (McMullan, 2002)	Join a rowdy New York City garbage truck on his rounds. If your students enjoy this book, read *I'm Mighty* (2003) and *I'm Dirty* (2006).	Voice Unique Use of Conventions
In November (Rylant, 2000)	Rylant's poetic language paints a vivid picture of November happenings.	Sentence Fluency/ Word Choice
The Night I Followed the Dog (Laden, 1994)	A boy details his adventures following his dog to the exclusive "dog club."	Unique Use of Conventions
No! That's Wrong! (Ji, 2008)	Rabbit finds a pair of underwear and thinks that the panties are a hat. An unknown narrator disagrees.	Voice
A Plump and Perky Turkey (Bateman, 2004)	The folks of Squawk Valley try to trick the turkey into being their meal.	Sentence Fluency
Snow Music (Perkins, 2003)	The music of a snowy day is cleverly captured in this interactive tale.	Sentence Fluency Unique Use of Conventions
Winter Is the Warmest Season (Stringer, 2006)	Stringer's flowing text celebrates the joys of winter. Students could write about why summer is the coldest season.	Ideas
Winter White (Jones, 2008)	One of ten books in the Know Your Colors series. In this book, the author uses a variety of adjectives to describe white winter items.	Grammar Word Choice
You Can Write a Story! (Bullard, 2007)	Bullard details the ingredients and steps to writing a fictional story. This "how-to" book is filled with a wealth of ideas and examples.	Organization

Part 2: A Menu of Mini-Lessons—Studying Story Elements

You might ask, "Why spend three months exploring stories?" That is an excellent question! We believe that when students understand how stories work, they not only become better writers, but they also become better readers. Learning how to create a memorable character strengthens their knowledge of how characters behave and change in the books they read. In addition, students use their knowledge of story elements to retell stories and demonstrate understanding. Finally, stories are a familiar and appealing genre for young learners that often gets neglected as they progress through the grades and the focus shifts to written responses and content area report writing. So we offer this opportunity for an in-depth study. Of course, if your students are ready to move on to other genres, skip ahead to explore letter writing, poetry, or nonfiction!

MINI-LESSON: WHAT KIND OF LEAD DO I NEED?

PREPARATION: Collect picture books that represent different types of beginning sentences. We've provided three leads of each type so that you can use the same mini-lesson at various grade levels with different picture books. To collect leads as a whole class, create a chart entitled "What Kind of Lead Do

What Kind of Lead Do I Need?	
Character Leads	
Farmer Brown has a problem.	Click, Clack, Moo: Cows That Type (Cronin, 2000)
Pirates have green teeth—when they have any teeth at all.	How I Became a Pirate (Long, 2003)
Sure, she was little, but Beatrice loved riddles and tricks and she could think fast on her feet.	Clever Beatrice (Willey, 2001)
Quotation Leads	
"Help, I've been robbed!" We heard Grandpa shouting.	Grandpa's Teeth (Clement, 1997)
"Ho hum," yawned Mr. Tortoise. "Winter is here."	A Silly Snowy Day (Coleman, 2000)
"I can't wait! I can't wait!" said Arthur.	Arthur's Birthday (Brown, 1989)
Setting Leads	
After the war, there was little left in the tiny Dutch town of Olst.	Boxes for Katje (Fleming, 2003)
In a warm and sultry forest far, far away, there once lived a mother fruit bat and her new baby.	Stellaluna (Cannon, 1993)
It was cold outside. It was warm inside. A fine day for gingerbread, Matti thought.	Gingerbread Baby (Brett, 1999)

I Need?" Supply each of your writers with a sticky note to mark a place in their writer's notebook to collect leads. For second-grade writers, create a booklet with a separate page for each type of lead. Then, provide time for them to locate and categorize the opening lines of their favorite tales.

EXPLANATION: The beginning lines of a story are designed to grab your attention and compel you to keep reading. Pointing out the techniques authors use to start a book raises students' awareness of the choices they have as writers.

DEMONSTRATION: Model composing a few different leads for the piece you are currently writing.

INVITATION: "Writers, today during writing workshop I want you to experiment with writing various types of leads. If you get stuck, go to our classroom library and look at how some of your favorite books begin. Feel free to record and collect some of those ideas in your writing workshop folder."

MINI-LESSON: QUESTIONING THE CHARACTER

PREPARATION: Prepare a chart entitled "Questioning the Character."

EXPLANATION: The aim of this mini-lesson is to provide students with a concrete way to conceive a character using a series of questions. Once students are familiar with the questioning strategy, they can apply it whenever they are creating characters.

DEMONSTRATION: Launch the mini-lesson by saying, "Let's put our heads together to create a list of questions that we might ask ourselves about a character." Record student responses on a chart. After the chart is complete, model writing about a character by answering the questions.

INVITATION: "Authors, as you are creating characters for your stories, refer to the Questioning the Character chart as you bring your character to life."

MINI-LESSON: USING SIMILES TO DESCRIBE A CHARACTER

PREPARATION: Read and discuss *My Dog Is as Smelly as Dirty Socks* (Piven, 2007). This clever book contains family portraits created from everyday objects coupled with descriptions written in similes.

> ### Questioning the Character
>
> What is your name?
> What do you look like?
> How old are you?
> Where do you live?
> Who is in your family?
> What are your hobbies?
> What is your favorite food?
> Who are your friends?
> What do you like to do?

EXPLANATION: Piven's book models another way to describe a character—by using similes. This mini-lesson lends itself to a teacher-guided writing activity.

DEMONSTRATION: After reading aloud, make a two-column chart with the headings "I'm . . ." and "Object." Brainstorm a list of words to describe a person, and then elicit input from your students to think of objects that match the descriptive words, or show children objects and create a list of descriptive words. To differentiate for kindergarten, consider using animals rather than objects. Then write a self-description using Piven's model:

> I'm as _____ as a _____. That's me! (Repeat the process with different self-descriptions as needed until children grasp the concept.)

INVITATION: "Writers, now it's your turn. I'm going to give you some paper to make a two-column chart. Record five words to describe yourself and one object to match each descriptive word. Tomorrow we will use these words to help us write our own descriptions."

I'm . . .	Object
funny	comic strip
smart	book
tough	rock
hungry	fork
loud	drum
tiny	ant
confused	puzzle
thirsty	mug
fast	rollerblade
tired	pillow

MINI-LESSON: INTRODUCING ADJECTIVES—AN ALPHABET OF ADJECTIVES

PREPARATION: Read and discuss a colorful concept book that highlights adjectives, such as:

> *A Is for Angry: An Animal and Adjective Alphabet* (Boynton, 1987)
>
> *Hairy, Scary, Ordinary: What Is an Adjective?* (Cleary, 2000)
>
> *If You Were an Adjective* (Dahl, 2006)

EXPLANATION: In the previous two chapters, you introduced nouns and verbs. Many of this chapter's mini-lessons rely on an understanding of adjectives. To this end, we offer this introductory lesson to help students grasp the purpose of adjectives.

DEMONSTRATION: Any of the books listed in the preparation section will be helpful in introducing adjectives and then creating an adjective collection. For your demonstration, show writers how and where you would like them to collect adjectives. We used an "Alphabox" chart (Hoyt, 1999, p. 17) to organize our collection.

INVITATION: "Wow, writers, you have a lot of adjectives to choose from. We will continue adding to our collection as the year goes on."

MINI-LESSON: SETTINGS AND SENSES

PREPARATION: Read and discuss *Hello Ocean* (Ryan, 2001), in which the author uses the five senses to vividly describe the ocean.

EXPLANATION: One of the keys to creating a memorable setting is to describe it using sensory details. Children will help you describe another setting as vividly as Pam Muñoz Ryan describes the ocean.

DEMONSTRATION: To begin, make a chart listing the senses. Collaborate to write key words and phrases to help with your descriptive piece. The next day, work together in a shared writing format to pen a description of the setting.

An Alphabet of Adjectives

A angry	B bashful bold	C clean	D dirty	E energetic	F frightened fancy fiery
G grumpy gigantic	H hungry huge handsome	I ill	J jazzy	K kind	L loud
M mighty	N nosy	O outraged	P playful pretty prissy	Q quick	R rotund
S sleepy scary scaly strong	T tangled tough	U upside-down	V vain	WX wide	YZ young zany

Begin an alphabetically organized adjective collection.

HELLO OCEAN

Pam Muñoz Ryan
illustrated by Mark Astrella

SETTING	See	Hear	Taste/Smell	Touch/Feel
Jungle	thick grass bright sun	screeching monkeys	tropical fruits mossy trees	humid air scratching vines sweaty
Desert	golden sand coyotes	wind whistling rattlesnakes	gritty sand	dry air cactus (ouch!) hot

INVITATION: "As you reread your work, look for places where you can add sensory details about your setting so that your readers will feel as if they are there."

MINI-LESSON: CHUNK IT! A STRATEGY FOR SPELLING MULTISYLLABIC WORDS 🦉

PREPARATION:

- Compile a list of multisyllabic words, including words such as *misunderstanding, sickness, fantastic, sportsmanship, interesting, transporter, grandmother, chickenpox, candlestick, mathematics, vocabulary, stingray,* and *lumberjack.*
- Cut squares of paper to record the chunks of the words.

EXPLANATION: This mini-lesson targets spellers who are ready to apply their phonics knowledge to longer words. This strategy is helpful in both writing and reading.

DEMONSTRATION: Begin with an explanation such as "Today before I continue my writing, I want to think about what writers do when they have to spell a long word." Begin with a word on your list. Say the word as you normally would. Next, say it and have students join you in clapping the syllables of the word. Ask students to help you write the letters that match each syllable on a paper square. For example, the word *fantastic* would be written on three squares: <u>fan</u>-<u>tas</u>-<u>tic</u>. Continue in the same fashion with a few more words, and then resume your modeling.

INVITATION: "Today while you are writing, remember to listen for the chunks in those long words. That's what writers do."

MINI-LESSON: CAN YOU COMBINE THESE SENTENCES? 🎵

PREPARATION:

- Write the short sample sentences (page 85) onto sentence strips; do not copy the combined sentences (the third in each set).
- Gather 12" x 18" sheets of white paper.

EXPLANATION: In an article published in *The Reading Teacher* (2005), Professor Bruce Saddler offers a helpful idea to practice combining short sentences into longer, more fluent ones. To kick off this lesson, explain that you are going to show students how writers create interesting sentences that sound good to their readers. For our youngest writers, Saddler suggests beginning with "cued" practice, meaning the clue word is underlined.

DEMONSTRATION: "Writers, today I am going to show you how to play the sentence-combining game." Begin by modeling a few sample sentences on the chalkboard or chart paper. Show students how to insert the underlined adjective before the noun in the sentence. Once students understand how to combine the two sentences, pair them up and give each duo a pair of sample sentences from the chart on the next page and a sheet of 12" x 18" paper.

Sample Sentences		
The pencil was yellow. The pencil was <u>sharp</u>. The sharp pencil was yellow.	The glue is white. The glue is <u>sticky</u>. The sticky glue is white.	The children were smart. The children were <u>funny</u>. The funny children were smart.
The classroom looks busy. The classroom looks <u>colorful</u>. The colorful classroom looks busy.	The book was exciting. The book was <u>informational</u>. The informational book was exciting.	Our teacher is kind. Our teacher is <u>helpful</u>. Our helpful teacher is kind.
The pizza is cheesy. The pizza has <u>pepperoni</u>. The pepperoni pizza is cheesy.	My cat is furry. My cat is <u>lazy</u>. My lazy cat is furry.	Our dog is barking. Our dog is <u>huge</u>. Our huge dog is barking.
The leaves are brown. The leaves are <u>crunchy</u>. The crunchy leaves are brown.	The turkey tasted juicy. The turkey looked <u>plump</u>. The plump turkey tasted juicy.	The snow is fluffy. The snow is <u>white</u>. The white snow is fluffy.
The tree is decorated. The tree is <u>beautiful</u>. The beautiful tree is decorated.	The cookies smell delicious. The cookies are <u>sweet</u>. The sweet cookies smell delicious.	The snowman is smiling. The snowman is <u>tall</u>. The tall snowman is smiling.

INVITATION: "Let's combine a sentence with our partner. Fold your paper in half. Begin by each writing one of the sentences in a space at the top of the page. Then, combine the sentence by inserting the underlined adjective before the noun, and write it at the bottom of the page. Once you are finished, you may illustrate your individual sentences and team up to illustrate the combined sentence."

MINI-LESSON: CREATING AN ADJECTIVE CHART USING A THESAURUS

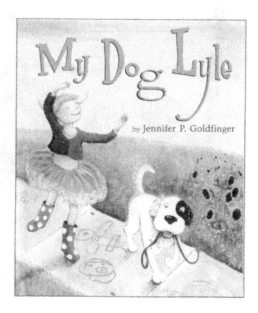

PREPARATION: Read and discuss either of these adjective-filled texts:

That's My Dog! (Walton, 2001). Children meet a big, red, happy, muddy, smart, bouncy, slobbery, sneaky, stinky dog.

My Dog Lyle (Goldfinger, 2007). Similar to *That's My Dog!*, this book features a girl who tells you all the reasons her dog is special.

EXPLANATION: The aim of this lesson is to initiate an

ongoing conversation about using precise adjectives. The chart will serve as a reusable resource for young writers.

DEMONSTRATION: Using a thesaurus, work with your students to create an adjective chart. Once the chart is complete, choose a person or animal to describe, and collaborate with your students in a shared or interactive writing format to rewrite the book read for this activity, using words from the adjective chart. See examples below.

Shape	Size	Color	Texture	Weight	Personality
square	colossal	golden	slimy	flimsy	sly
rounded	miniscule	fuchsia	furry	light	fierce
long	gigantic	crimson	scaly	heavy	joyful
thin	massive	carroty	spongy	wispy	friendly
triangular	teeny	violet	jagged	hefty	gloomy

INVITATION: "Writers, we are going to do some teacher-guided writing today. I want you to think of a book character that you know a lot about. Let's use the pattern found in the book to help us out."

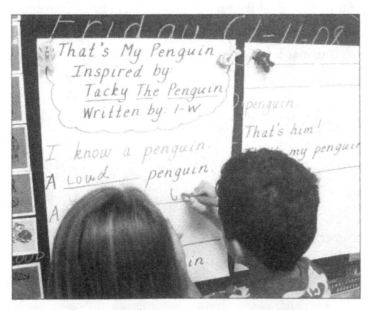

An interactive writing chart

Month-by-Month Trait-Based Writing Instruction

MINI-LESSON: DIFFERENT VERSIONS = DIFFERENT VOICES

PREPARATION: Locate a pairing or two of traditional tales, one a more traditional version and one a voice-filled retelling. (See chart, right.)

EXPLANATION: By comparing different versions of the same traditional tales, children will hear similar stories told with two very different voices.

DEMONSTRATION: Read the traditional version. Discuss or chart any observations about the form or content of the text. Next, read the voice-filled retelling and do the same.

Traditional Tale Pairings	
Traditional Version	**Voice-Filled Retelling**
The Gingerbread Boy (Galdone, 1975)	*The Gingerbread Cowboy* (Squires, 2006)
The Little Red Hen (Galdone, 1973)	*Armadilly Chili* (Ketteman, 2004) *Mañana, Iguana* (Paul, 2004)
Rapunzel (Ehrlich, 1989)	*Falling for Rapunzel* (Wilcox, 2003)

INVITATION: "Today we are going to connect our reading and writing with a teacher-guided writing idea. Choose a pair of tales and explain in words which tale you enjoyed more and why."

MINI-LESSON: IDENTIFYING EVENTS IN MENTOR TEXTS

PREPARATION: Select a few books that follow this pattern: The main character makes three attempts to solve his or her problem before succeeding. See the chart on page 88 for a few examples.

EXPLANATION: When talented children's author Candace Fleming helps students create a story, she uses a secret formula she's dubbed C.L.A.P.S. The clever acronym serves as a graphic organizer for students by reminding them that a story must include Characters, Location, Action, Problem, and Solution. For more information and lessons on using C.L.A.P.S., see *Literature Is Back! Using the Best Books for Teaching Readers and Writers Across Genres* (Fuhler & Walther, 2007). In many children's books, the character makes three different attempts to solve the problem. Typically, once these two attempts fail, the final attempt solves the problem.

DEMONSTRATION: The best way to show children how this works is to read examples from children's books and chart or discuss your findings.

INVITATION: "Story writers, to add action and detail to your story, go back and see what else your characters could do to try to solve their problem."

Badger's Fancy Meal (Kazsa, 2007)	**The Gruffalo** (Donaldson, 1999)
Somebody: Badger	**Somebody**: Mouse
wanted to eat	**wanted** to stroll through the woods
but instead of the same old meal, he wanted a fancy meal	**but** the animals wanted to eat him
so he tried to make a mole taco but the mole slipped away	**so** he tricked fox
	so he tricked owl
so he tried to make a rat burger but the rat wiggled away	**so** he tricked snake
	Finally, he tricked the Gruffalo
so he tried to make a rabbit banana split but the rabbit jumped away	**In the end**, all was quiet in the deep dark wood.
Finally, mole ended up at home	
In the end, the animals ate Badger's meal!	
Muncha! Muncha! Muncha! (Fleming, 2002)	**My Lucky Day** (Kasza, 2003)
Somebody: Mr. McGreely	**Somebody**: Fox
wanted to grow yummy vegetables	**wanted** to eat the piglet
but three hungry bunnies kept eating them	**but** piglet tricked fox
so Mr. McGreely built a small wire fence	**so** fox gave piglet a nice bath,
so Mr. McGreely built a tall wooden wall	**so** fox made piglet a nice dinner
so Mr. McGreely built a deep wet trench	**so** fox gave piglet a terrific massage
Finally, Mr. McGreely built a huge enormous thing	**Finally**, fox passed out
In the end, the bunnies tricked Mr. McGreely!	**In the end**, piglet thought, "Who shall I visit next?"

MINI-LESSON: ADD VOICE TO YOUR ILLUSTRATIONS WITH SPEECH BUBBLES 🗩

PREPARATION: Share a book in which the author uses speech bubbles to enhance or tell the story, such as one of those listed on the chart on page 89.

Books Brimming With Speech Bubbles	
Title and Author	**Brief Summary**
Best Buds (Eaton, 2007)	A boy named Max is worried when his best friend, Pinky the pig, disappears.
Leaving the Nest (Gerstein, 2007)	This lively story is set in a backyard where animals are all trying to "leave the nest." Each creature's thoughts and conversations are told through speech bubbles.
Superhero ABC (McLeod, 2006)	Humorous superheroes, both male and female, represent each letter of the alphabet.
Superheroes (Eaton, 2007)	Max and Pinky are back—determined to become superheroes.

EXPLANATION: Once children see how a small detail such as a speech bubble adds voice to an illustration and complements the writing, they will begin to incorporate speech bubbles into their own work.

DEMONSTRATION: Discuss the author's use of speech bubbles. Model the use of speech bubbles in your own illustrations. It is helpful to show students how to write the words first, and then surround the words with the bubble.

INVITATION: "Writers, as you are illustrating, use a speech bubble or two to enhance your ideas and give your illustrations voice."

MINI-LESSON: THE BIG ENDING

PREPARATION: Collect picture books that represent engaging conclusions. We've provided a sampling of creative last lines (see chart on next page). To collect conclusions as a whole class, create a chart entitled "The Big Ending!" You may want to supply your writers with sticky notes to mark a place in their writer's notebook to collect conclusions.

EXPLANATION: A satisfying ending ties up the story and typically occurs when the problem is solved. Following the ending, readers often find a conclusion or "big ending." It is an added line or two, often humorous, that authors use to conclude their piece. The conclusion is like the cherry on top of a delicious hot fudge sundae: The sundae tastes yummy without it—but the bright red cherry adds a little pizzazz!

DEMONSTRATION: Model composing a few different endings for the piece you are currently writing.

INVITATION: "Authors, today during writing workshop I want you to experiment with writing

The Big Ending		
And from that day forward, the prairie dogs lived happily—and fuzzlessly—ever after.	JANET STEVENS and SUSAN STEVENS CRUMMEL THE GREAT FUZZ FRENZY	The Great Fuzz Frenzy (Stevens & Stevens Crummel, 2005)
And that's how Hilda Mae Heifer got back her moo. Everyone else got earplugs.		Moo Who? (Palatini, 2004)
And that is the true story of Owen and Mzee, two great friends.		Owen & Mzee (Hatkoff, Hatkoff, & Kahumbu, 2006)
Backhoe Loader, signing off. Have a dirty day!		I'm Dirty! (McMullan, 2006)
"I do!" said the Page when the moon shone bright, and then he pulled the plug. Glub, glub, glub!		King Bidgood's in the Bathtub (Wood, 1985)
Tacky was an odd bird, but a very nice bird to have around.		Tacky the Penguin (Lester, 1988)

various types of endings. If you get stuck, go to our classroom library and look to see how some of your favorite books end. Feel free to record and collect a few of those ideas in your writing workshop folder."

MINI-LESSON: EXCLAMATION MARKS .?!

PREPARATION: Read *Hurry! Hurry!* (Bunting, 2007) aloud to the class.

EXPLANATION: Certainly, during read-aloud or at some point during your modeling, a discussion of exclamation marks and their purpose has already occurred. The goal of this mini-lesson is to highlight Eve Bunting's clever use of exclamation marks to make the story come alive.

DEMONSTRATION: Read the text of the book aloud without showing illustrations and with no expression. Discuss the students' reactions

to your reading. Reread *Hurry! Hurry!* with expression, this time showing the illustrations and predicting as you go. Again, discuss the students' observations and the differences between the two readings.

INVITATION: "Wow, the use of an exclamation mark really signals your reader to read that part with excitement! Look for a place in your piece where you could add an exclamation mark."

A young writer uses exclamation marks.

Part 3: Genre Exploration: Crafting a Story— The Elements

EXPLANATION

Building on the basics writers gained last month, the goal here is for the stories to be a bit longer and more detailed. If you choose to begin with a graphic organizer, we've included a few different story element planning sheets in Appendix A10 on page 182. Certainly, for some students, a planning sheet is helpful, but others may choose to simply begin drafting and then revise as they go. Your demonstrations and guidance during individual and small-group conferences will provide the support students need to craft a creative story. (See Genre Exploration Chart on next page.)

Final Thoughts

During the past two months, your students have discovered that the elements of a story are the essential ingredients for creating more elaborate, detailed tales. As the year continues and you and your students explore other genres, you will continue to build on this foundation as you read aloud books published either by an adult author or one of your own famous classroom writers. Each read-aloud offers an opportunity to point out or ask students to notice a tip, trick, or technique that the author employed that may someday become part of your students' writing repertoire.

November & December Genre Exploration Chart
Crafting a Story: The Elements

Kid-Friendly Definition of Genre: A story is when you tell someone about something that has happened. It can be real or make-believe.

Characteristics of Genre:
- Main character can be the writer or another person or creature.
- Author uses his or her imagination to create the tale.
- Written in either first person or third person.
- Narrates a chain of related events.
- Contains characters, setting, action, problem, events, and solution.
- Uses sensory details to describe things.

Mentor Texts		
K	**1**	**2**
Breakfast for Jack (Schories, 2004) *Jack and the Missing Piece* (Schories, 2004) *Jack and the Night Visitors* (Schories, 2006) These wordless picture books introduce the youngest learners to characters, setting, and action.	See mini-lesson Identifying Events in Mentor Texts on pages 87–88 for a list of mentor texts.	*Aunt Isabel Tells a Good One* (Duke, 1992) Penelope and Aunt Isabel craft a story with all the right ingredients.

Zooming In to Align Instruction Across the Grades		
K—Eventful Fiction	**1—An Elemental Tale**	**2—Adding Interesting Ingredients**
• As you model and students plan their own stories, consider these words: Who? Is Doing What? Where? How Does Your Story End?	• Students use the acronym C.L.A.P.S.—representing Characters, Location, Action, Problem, Solution (Fuhler & Walther, 2007)—to guide their make-believe story writing.	• The "graphic organizer" provided in the book *Aunt Isabel Tells a Good One* (Duke, 1992) encourages writers to include romance, a villain, and danger in their stories.

Chapter 5

January: Discovering Real-World Genres

Happy New Year!

A new year. One of the many appealing aspects of being a teacher is that we get two chances at a fresh start each year. One occurs in the fall when our students arrive, and the other opportunity emerges in January. While the rest of our friends are dusting off their treadmills, we have a chance to renew our efforts at school (*and* get back to the gym!). Before the pace picks up again, reflect on the teaching and learning that have occurred thus far. Take a moment to celebrate the progress your students have made as writers. Use the data you have gathered from your formal and informal assessments to set goals for the second half of the school year. Then, take a deep breath and get ready to jump back in. This month we will turn our attention to the types of writing students will encounter and use in their daily lives. We call these the "real-world genres." In this chapter you will find lessons that guide students as they compose letters, notes, lists, recipes, and more.

Part 1: Morning Message Ideas and Samples

After winter break, kids are ready for the challenge of thinking about and writing some different kinds of texts. For this reason, we begin the new year with morning messages that review, reinforce, or extend students' understanding of real-world genres. Likewise, the messages continue to build students' awareness of grammar and conventions with a focus on singular and plural nouns, past- and present-tense verbs, and the use of commas. Enjoy teaching writing essentials to your students, one message at a time!

MORNING MESSAGE IDEA: JANUARY WORD CHART

See explanation on page 35.

MORNING MESSAGE IDEA: REAL-WORLD WRITING

In her book *Snapshots* (2000, p. 230), Linda Hoyt has a lesson called "Note Writing and List Making," in which she details all of the reasons that she writes. This lesson is easily adapted to the morning message. Instead of listing all the different ways and reasons you write, prompt students to notice and name the types of writing they see people doing. On Monday, pose the question, "What kinds of things do you see people writing?" Ask children to pay attention to people who are writing at school, at home, and around town. Post a chart near your meeting area to collect ideas during the week. Draw attention to the occasions when you are writing by pausing to

Morning Message Sample

January Word Chart

snowman	sledding	ice skating
winter	snowflakes	gloves
new year	resolution	blustery
speech	parade	jacket

Martin Luther King, Jr.

Morning Message Sample

Real-World Writing

What kinds of things do you see people writing?

Who?	What?	Why?
dad	e-mail	to ask a question about his job
mom	a note to my teacher	to explain why I'm leaving early
brother	an essay	to tell about the book he just finished
teacher	a note to the nurse	to ask her for more bandage strips

discuss what you are writing and the purpose for that particular type of writing. At the end of the week, categorize the different types of writing.

MORNING MESSAGE IDEA: LET'S WRITE A LIST

Once you have introduced the process of list writing in the mini-lesson on page 100, encourage children to write lists for a variety of purposes. For those students who find generating ideas a challenge, a list is a helpful organizational tool when settling on a topic for writing. Children can also create lists to enhance their word choice by listing the vivid color names found on their crayons. As you are writing lists in a shared or interactive writing format, model the different conventions used to signal a list, such as numbers, bullets, and dashes.

Below are a few samples to spark ideas.

Morning Message: Making a list of our favorite characters

Morning Message Sample

Let's Write a List

Let's write a list of . . .

Settings	Favorite Characters	Winter Nouns
1. Cave	• Clementine	– snowman
2. Treehouse	• Jigsaw Jones	– hat
3. School		– scarf
4. Wrigley Field	• George and Martha	– ice
5. Museum	• Fly Guy	– boots
	• Fancy Nancy	

MORNING MESSAGE IDEA: THE LETTER STEALER— WORD ENDINGS

See explanation on page 39.

Morning Message Sample

The Letter Stealer—Word Endings

Yesterday we learn___ about how Martin Luther King, Jr. march__ and gave speech___. He was an amaz____ man! (Yesterday we learned about how Martin Luther King, Jr., marched and gave speeches. He was an amazing man!)

MORNING MESSAGE IDEA: A FRIENDLY LETTER

As students learn about and craft friendly letters, the morning message offers a venue for continually reinforcing the concepts you have introduced and explored during your mini-lessons. To review and practice the conventions in general and the specific conventions of a friendly letter, write letters to or with your students, leaving out the punctuation in the body, greeting, and closing.

> **Morning Message Sample**
>
> **A Friendly Letter**
>
> Dear First Graders
>   I learned a lot on our field trip yesterday What did you learn What part of the trip did you like the best I can't wait to go on our next field trip to the rock museum
>   Your teacher
>   Ms. Phillips

MORNING MESSAGE IDEA: WORD EXCHANGE

See explanation on page 37.

> **Morning Message Sample**
>
> **Word Exchange**
>
> Let's make a word exchange! What are the different ways to close a friendly letter?

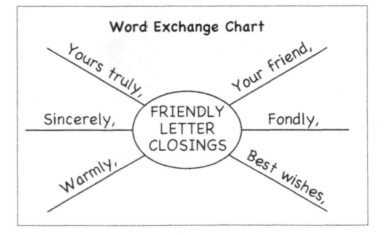

Word Exchange Chart

Yours truly, Your friend, Sincerely, FRIENDLY LETTER CLOSINGS Fondly, Warmly, Best wishes,

MORNING MESSAGE IDEA: SINGULAR AND PLURAL NOUNS

For some students, the addition of the letter(s) *s* or *es* at the end of nouns to make them plural happens naturally as they become more adept at writing. For others, including English language learners, the use of the plural *s* or *es* is problematic. To initiate a conversation about singular and plural nouns, write either a sampling of sentences or a message leaving off the ending *s* or *es*. Ask children, "Do these sentences sound right?" As you read and edit the words, discuss why it is important to add an *s* or *es* and what clues in the sentence indicate that an *s* or *es* is needed.

Morning Message Sample

Singular and Plural Nouns

What is missing from these sentences?	What is wrong with this message?
The three bear live in the woods. Yikes! A swarm of bee is chasing me. Our library has many book.	It is a cold day. Do you have a hat, two boot, and a pair of mitten?

MORNING MESSAGE IDEA: PAST- AND PRESENT-TENSE VERBS

We're sure you've noticed that until students have had plenty of practice, they encounter difficulty decoding the *–ed* endings in their reading. Some read words such as *walked* as "walk-ed" or *talked* as "talk-ed." If you observe students making these miscues, you may want to incorporate this message into your repertoire. The more opportunities students have to locate errors and correct grammatical slip-ups with a knowledgeable teacher at their side, the more likely they are to notice similar mistakes in their own writing. To facilitate this message, read each sentence as it is written. Then, invite students to correct the verbs while discussing the words that signal the past tense.

Morning Message Sample

Past- and Present-Tense Verbs

Last night I frost the cake.

Yesterday my teacher stamp the paper.

Last summer my bike rust in the rain.

In 1969, the rocket blast off and land on the round-shape moon.

MORNING MESSAGE IDEA: COMMAS IN A SERIES

Thank goodness for commas. They are an easy solution to a common problem that young writers encounter called "and-itis." See the mini-lesson on page 105 for further explanation of "and-itis." For this message, prewrite a sentence including a lot of *ands*. Read the sentence chorally, and then demonstrate how to replace the *ands*

Morning Message Sample

Commas in a Series

My snowman has a hat and a carrot nose and a scarf and black buttons.

Rewritten sentence:
My snowman has a hat, a carrot nose, a scarf, and black buttons.

with commas. Rewrite in an interactive format and together replace the *ands* with commas. Introduce the term "commas in a series" so that students begin to notice and name this convention in their own writing.

MORNING MESSAGE IDEA: WHO WILL RECEIVE THIS LETTER? 💬

The act of letter writing is one effective way to teach the concept of voice because the tone and word choice of a letter change based on its audience and purpose. For this message, collect authentic letters from school or home and post them on the board. After reading the letters, ask students if they can determine the recipient of the letter based on the voice. Another alternative is to create letters of your own similar to the samples shown above.

Morning Message Sample

Who Will Receive This Letter?

Dear (Stink),
    I can't believe you got to go to Washington, D.C., without me! Just wait till you get home. I have a big surprise for you. ROAR!
          Your sister,
          Judy Moody

Dear _____ (Principal's Name) _____,
    This letter is to inform you that the students would like to have an additional 15 minutes of recess per day. The research shows that exercise is good for their bodies and brains.

          Sincerely,
          Dr. Walther

WRITING WORKSHOP TIP:
Maintaining Balance Between Student Choice and Teacher-Guided Writing

As you preview the mini-lessons in this chapter, notice that many of the examples will take a few days to complete and are followed by a "teacher-guided" invitation. Carefully select topics you want to teach this month to ensure a balance between student-selected writing time and teacher-guided invitations. In addition, you may have a few mini-lessons you want to revisit from previous chapters. To guide your decision-making and coordinate your writing program across grade levels, have a discussion with your colleagues at other grade levels to determine the best level to focus on a particular genre or aspect of writing. Perhaps kindergarten teachers will focus on lists, while first-grade teachers will spend more time on notes and introducing friendly letters, and second-grade instruction will emphasize the architecture of a persuasive letter.

Read-Alouds for Writers		
Title and Author	**Brief Summary**	**Focus**
All You Need for a Snowman (Schertle, 2002)	A rhythmic wintry tale with perfect pauses for predicting	Sentence Fluency
Chicken Soup by Heart (Hershenhorn, 2002)	Rudie cooks a batch of chicken soup using Mrs. Gittel's secret recipe—stories!	Ideas
The First Day of Winter (Fleming, 2005)	Using the tune from "The Twelve Days of Christmas," Fleming creates a cumulative tale about decorating a snowman.	Sentence Fluency Word Choice
Freedom on the Menu (Weatherford, 2005)	Connie's first-person account of the Greensboro sit-ins offers an age-appropriate, insider's view of the civil rights era.	Voice
Martin's Big Words (Rappaport, 2001)	A tribute to Dr. King with a sampling of quotes from his writing and speeches	Word Choice
The Mitten (Brett, 1989)	Students could use the pattern from this folktale to craft their own version.	Ideas
The Snow Show (Fisher, 2008)	"Welcome to The Snow Show!" where Chef Kelvin and Jack Frost cook up a fresh batch of snow. This clever book, written like a recipe, describes the steps in making snow. Funny anecdotes in the illustrations are sure to keep readers interested.	Organization
Snow Sounds: An Onomatopoeic Story (Johnson, 2006)	Descriptive words accent the visual narrative in this nearly wordless book about wintry weather.	Word Choice
Snowmen at Night (Buehner, 2002)	A bouncy, rhyming text details the evening adventures of snowmen.	Sentence Fluency
Tacky the Penguin (Lester, 1988)	Winter wouldn't be the same without reading the books from the Tacky series!	Voice

Part 2: A Menu of Mini-Lessons—Writing in the Real World

In an effort to provide students with a well-rounded view of writing, we offer the mini-lessons in this chapter. The goal is for children to recognize that being a writer means more than writing a narrative text. As you emphasize the fact that writers make deliberate choices about how they will communicate their ideas, based on their purpose and audience, you broaden students' definition of writing.

MINI-LESSON: JOT IT DOWN!

PREPARATION: Share the book *Giggle, Giggle, Quack* (Cronin, 2002). When Farmer Brown goes on vacation, he leaves his brother Bob some helpful notes. But the sneaky duck replaces them with notes of his own.

EXPLANATION: A note is a short, informal way to communicate a brief message in writing. The aim of this lesson is to teach students the purposes for and elements of a note and then encourage them to write notes for authentic purposes. For example, if you are working with a student or a small group and a child tries to interrupt, simply signal them to write you a note. Certainly, it is essential to model and practice this routine prior to putting it into daily practice. In addition, provide an easy-to-access supply of note paper (see Appendix A11, page 183) and a designated spot for students to post their notes. To manage student-to-student note writing, make a centralized mailbox so that you can quickly glance at the content of the notes before they are passed on to the child.

DEMONSTRATION: Say, "Farmer Brown and the duck wrote a lot of notes. Let's take a look at them again to see what they look like." Jot down students' thoughts. "Today I'm going to write a note to Ms. Phillips asking her if I can borrow a book. Let's see; I'll begin by writing her name, and then continue with my message. . . ."

INVITATION: "Girls and boys, today before you get back to your own writing, I'd like you to try your hand at writing a note. You may choose to write a note to another student in our classroom or jot down a note to me."

MINI-LESSON: LET'S WRITE A LIST

PREPARATION:

- Launch your mini-lesson by rereading the list portions of any of the books in the box on page 101 or reading a few real-world lists, such as your grocery list, a list of students' names, and so on.

Books That Include Lists	
Title and Author	**Brief Summary**
Diary of a Worm (Cronin, 2003) *Diary of a Spider* (Cronin, 2005)	These books are ideal for kindergarten because Worm and Spider each write short lists containing three ideas.
Frog and Toad Together (Lobel, 1972)	In the chapter entitled "The List," Toad writes a list of the things he has to do.
Wallace's Lists (Bottner & Kruglik, 2004)	Wallace the mouse lives his life by lists until his neighbor Albert urges him to experience adventures not on his lists.

- Reproduce a supply of list paper (see Appendix A11, page 183).

EXPLANATION: Lists are one type of real-world writing that students will use throughout their lives. Why not take a few days to explore the characteristics of list-making?

DEMONSTRATION: Before modeling how to create a list of your own, make a chart of possible list topics. Think of ideas linked to your current units of study. Some curricular-related topics might include healthy foods, weather words, farm animals, planet names, "green" nouns, vivid verbs, story characters, and map features. Post the chart or copy it for students to keep in their writing folders. For your demonstration, pick a topic and then generate a list.

INVITATION: "Authors, today we are going to start writing time by writing a list. Once your list is complete, you may use it as a starting point for a new piece of writing, or you may tuck it into your folder to spark ideas in the future and continue working on your other writing."

MINI-LESSON: MAPPING IDEAS 🌐

PREPARATION: Read *My Map Book* (Fanelli, 1995), in which a girl creates a collection of unique maps, including a map of her heart. Notice all the different types of maps Sara designs, including maps about the food in her tummy, her day, her neighborhood, and her heart.

EXPLANATION: When we think of organization in writing, we often associate it with graphic organizers, story webs, outlines, or other structured formats. For young children, organization begins by sorting, categorizing, and arranging illustrations and words in a certain way on a page. Thus, the use of a map to organize ideas offers a unique visual medium to arrange similar ideas.

DEMONSTRATION: After reading, generate a list of concepts for young writers to map. The list might include a map of a creature, a planet, a story, a plant, Lincoln's life, a baseball field, and so on. Demonstrate the process of creating your own map.

INVITATION: "Writers, we are going to take a break from your student-choice writing and do some teacher-guided writing. To begin, decide what kind of map you would like to make. Once you've made that decision, jot a list of ideas that you might include on the map." After students have picked their maps and jotted their lists of ideas, provide each child with a blank piece of paper or preprinted shape to craft his or her own map. You may choose to have students revise, edit, and polish their maps to present on a bulletin board.

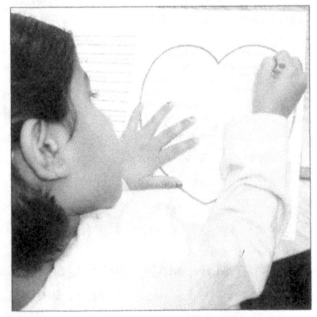

Students create a map of their heart.

MINI-LESSON: WRITE A BOOK BLURB 🔊

PREPARATION: Gather a stack of books with engaging back-cover blurbs. Read and discuss the common characteristics of a book blurb. Add students' observations to the Helpful Hints for Writing Blurbs anchor chart (at right).

EXPLANATION: Teaching children how to write a back-cover blurb not only helps them summarize their own stories, but it also raises their awareness of the helpful prereading strategy of reading the cover and back of the book.

DEMONSTRATION: For your demonstration, choose a familiar picture book that does not have a back-cover blurb. Model writing a blurb for that book. If you choose, you can rewrite the blurb on a sticky note and affix it to the book.

INVITATION: "Writers, now is your chance to write a blurb for a familiar book. Pick a book from the shelf that you have read that doesn't have a blurb and craft an inviting blurb to entice others to read that particular book." After students have had time to practice, ask them to choose their best effort, revise, edit, and display it with the book. Students can also write blurbs for their own books. See examples below.

> ### Helpful Hints for Writing Blurbs
>
> • Keep it short.
>
> • Tell readers enough to make them want to read the book.
>
> • Don't give away the ending.

This is a story about a girl named Abbey. She go [went] to Peoria. She went apple picking.

This story is about Christmas Day in 2001. My first Christmas a long time ago.

MINI-LESSON: THE ABCs OF ORGANIZATION 🌐

PREPARATION: Gather alphabet books with unique characteristics. As you read the books aloud, notice the different techniques the authors employ.

Alphabet Books With Unique Characteristics	
Title and Author	**Unique Characteristics**
Bad Kitty (Bruel, 2005)	Bruel uses the alphabet four times to help tell the story of Bad Kitty. Also, read *Poor Puppy* (Bruel, 2007).
Fancy Nancy's Favorite Fancy Words: From Accessories to Zany (O'Connor, 2008)	A vocabulary-boosting book featuring the fancy words, their definitions, and a sentence containing the word
Shiver Me Letters: A Pirate ABC (Sobel, 2006)	Pirate fans will enjoy this rhyming alphabet adventure.
S Is for Story: A Writer's Alphabet (Hershenhorn, 2009)	This book includes writing terms such as *character*, *edit*, *genre*, and *revision* and is an example of an alphabet book that truly educates.
Twenty-Six Princesses (Horowitz, 2008)	Rhyming verse and humorous cartoons create a unique royal alphabet book.

EXPLANATION: Alphabet books provide yet another way to summarize and organize information. Young authors can write an alphabet book of places to visit, Martin Luther King, Jr.'s, life, or things in the classroom or school.

DEMONSTRATION: The content of your demonstration will depend on whether you're going to guide students in making a class alphabet book, with each child writing a page, or an individual or small-group book with students creating multiple pages. To show students how to incorporate the techniques found in the mentor texts, include such techniques in the sample alphabet book pages you model.

INVITATION: "Wow, authors, we surely have learned a lot about alphabet books! Let's use what we've learned from the mentor texts to create our own alphabet book. Share with a neighbor the writing techniques you might include on your page."

MINI-LESSON: YIKES! I HAVE AND-ITIS!

PREPARATION: Write a story that's peppered with the word *and*, either on an overhead or a sheet of chart paper.

EXPLANATION: Use this mini-lesson to teach writers how to replace the word *and* with transition words or phrases.

DEMONSTRATION: Open this mini-lesson by saying, "Boys and girls, I have a terrible disease that some writers get, called *and-itis*." Then, share a piece of writing on the overhead. Continue, "When writers get this disease, they have a few options. First, they can cross out *and*, and then replace it with a period, or they can use 'connecting words.' Connecting words help build a bridge from one sentence to the next. Let's make a list of connecting words to help us next time we have *and-itis*."

INVITATION: "Editors, today your challenge is to be an *and* detective. Go back into your writing folder and find a piece of writing. Can you eliminate some of the *ands*?"

> Yesterday I went to my friend's birthday party and we went to Chuck E. Cheese and we played games and I won 300 tickets and we opened presents and we ate pizza and my friend blew out the candles and we ate chocolate cake and we had a marvelous time and we went home.

Thanks to Mary Dolan, second-grade teacher at Owen Elementary School, for sharing this engaging and effective mini-lesson!

MINI-LESSON: LET'S BUILD A SENTENCE

PREPARATION: Prepare a chart with a few sentence beginnings. See chart, next page.

EXPLANATION: We originally found this clever lesson in the book *Seeing With New Eyes: A Guidebook on Teaching and Assessing Beginning Writers* (1999), published by the Northwest Regional Educational Laboratory, and have added to and adapted it over the years. This mini-lesson is designed to illuminate the fact that sentences can begin in many different ways. So have fun, use your imagination, and look in books such as *Once Upon a Time, The End* (Kloske, 2005) to add to the list of sentence beginnings (p. 106).

The first page of this book includes a collection of different sentence beginnings.

Sample Sentence Beginnings

In the morning . . .	Through the woods . . .	When it was dark . . .
In a small house . . .	Across a great ocean . . .	Late at night . . .
In a land far away . . .	On a hill . . .	Under a full moon . . .
A long time ago . . .	This is a . . .	Crash! . . .
Here are some . . .	How would you . . .	Have you ever
Imagine that you . . .	After dark . . .	wondered . . .

DEMONSTRATION: To begin, invite students to choose a topic related to an area of study in your curriculum, such as penguins or polar bears. Read, write, or orally share a sentence beginning. After you say or write a beginning, challenge students to create an ending that completes the sentence. For example, if the topic is dogs, after you say/write, "In the morning," a child might add, "our dog barks." Next you say/write, "A long time ago," and another student finishes with "dogs were wild."

INVITATION: "Writers, I will leave this chart handy. As you are writing, think about your sentence fluency. Reread your words aloud. Do your sentences flow? Are you starting your sentences in different ways?"

MINI-LESSON: WRITE A FRIENDLY LETTER 💬 ?!

PREPARATION:

- Select a few books containing friendly letters to share with your students.
- Prior to reading, discuss the different purposes for letters by asking questions such as "What type of letter would you write if someone gave you a present? What type of letter would you write if you broke your friend's toy? What type of letter would you write if you were having a party?"
- After reading each book, discuss the characteristics of a friendly letter and record them on a chart (see right).

What Do Friendly Letters Look Like and Sound Like?

Looks Like:

Heading: includes address and date (Introduce in second grade)

Greeting,
   Body
      Closing,
      Signature
P.S.

Sounds Like:

- Talking to a friend
- Sharing news about your life
- Asking questions about your friend's life

Books That Contain Friendly Letters	
Title and Author	**Brief Summary**
Click, Clack, Moo: Cows That Type (Cronin, 2000)	The cows write letters to Farmer Brown, requesting electric blankets for themselves and the hens.
Dear Mrs. LaRue: Letters From Obedience School (Teague, 2002)	Ike sends letters to his owner from the Brotweiler Canine Academy.
Dear Peter Rabbit (Ada, 1994) *With Love, Little Red Hen* (Ada, 2001) *Yours Truly, Goldilocks* (Ada, 1998)	Learn more about familiar storybook characters through the charming letters they write to each other.
The Gardener (Stewart, 1997)	When Lydia Grace has to leave home to stay with her Uncle Jim in the city, her spirit and love for flowers brighten the bakery and shine through in her letters home.
Thea's Tree (Jackson, 2008)	After Thea plants a purple bean for her science project, she writes to experts to try to figure out what is happening in her front yard.

EXPLANATION: The point of this lesson is to teach the format and characteristics of a friendly letter.

DEMONSTRATION: Once you've introduced and explored the friendly letter format through read-aloud and discussion, demonstrate writing a letter to a colleague or friend. As you are modeling, discuss how knowing your audience and defining your purpose make writing a friendly letter different than, let's say, writing a letter to the President of the United States.

INVITATION: "Writers, today you might want to craft a friendly letter. You can write it to a real friend or to a book character you would like to befriend."

MINI-LESSON: PLAYING WITH PREPOSITIONS

PREPARATION: Read either *Rosie's Walk* (Hutchins, 1968) or *Around the House the Fox Chased the Mouse: A Prepositional Tale* (Walton, 2006). You may find the Hutchins book more engaging for kindergartners. Both authors weave prepositions throughout their action-packed tales.

EXPLANATION: The goal of this mini-lesson is to introduce writers to the concept of prepositions.

DEMONSTRATION: Say, "The author used prepositions to help write a story. Do you think we could write our own prepositional tale together? Let's give it a try!" Work in a shared or interactive writing format to create a humorous prepositional tale. It might be helpful to make a list of the prepositions for future use.

INVITATION: "Authors, if you are looking for a unique idea, perhaps you can use prepositions to create your own adventure!"

MINI-LESSON: A LETTER OF ADVICE TO A NURSERY RHYME CHARACTER

PREPARATION:

- Prior to this mini-lesson, acquaint your students with nursery rhyme characters by reading some books of familiar nursery rhymes. Two appealing titles are listed below:

    The Neat Line: Scribbling Through Mother Goose (Edwards, 2005). The "neat line" helps nursery rhyme characters solve some of their problems.

    The Neighborhood Mother Goose (Crews, 2004). An updated, photographic look at nursery rhymes set in Brooklyn

- In addition, you will want to discuss the concept of advice. A helpful resource for this discussion is *Help Me, Mr. Mutt!* (Stevens & Stevens Crummel, 2008), in which Mr. Mutt is an advice columnist for dogs with people problems.

- Finally, write the names of various nursery rhyme characters on cards—come up with enough names so each student can select a different character. Do not include the name of the character you will use for your own letter.

EXPLANATION: It is apparent that a number of the nursery rhyme characters have problems to solve. For instance, Mary's lamb is always following her around, Humpty falls off the wall, and Little Bo Peep loses her sheep.

DEMONSTRATION: Say, "Today I'm going to write a letter of advice to Humpty Dumpty. What does *advice* mean again?" Review the meaning of advice. "Good thinking! In my letter I'm going to give Humpty some suggestions on how to keep from falling off that wall." Proceed by modeling your friendly letter, pointing out the essential elements, such as greeting, body, and closing.

INVITATION: "For the next few days, I will guide you as you each write a letter of advice to a nursery rhyme character. Remember to look at the chart we made about friendly letters while you are writing."

MINI-LESSON: TO SQUISH OR NOT TO SQUISH—WRITE A PERSUASIVE LETTER 🌐

PREPARATION: Read and discuss *Hey, Little Ant* (Hoose & Hoose, 1998), a humorous song-based picture book of a conversation between a young boy and a tiny ant. Throughout the book, the boy is trying to decide whether he should squish the ant or not. The book ends with the question "What do you think that kid should do?"

EXPLANATION: The genre of persuasive writing is often found on standardized writing tests. This mini-lesson offers a first look at the genre.

DEMONSTRATION: After reading *Hey, Little Ant*, list the boy's two choices on chart paper. Under each choice, have students brainstorm compelling reasons for making that decision. Work with students in a shared writing format to draft a persuasive letter that argues for squishing the ant. Use the following guidelines:

- Address your audience.
- Include an appealing introduction.
- Detail reasons that convince the reader.

A letter of advice to Little Bo Peep

- State the action you would like the reader to take.
- Use powerful words.

INVITATION: "Writers, it's time to persuade the boy not to squish the ant. Craft a persuasive letter to convince him to let the ant go free."

MINI-LESSON: WRITE A RECIPE 🌐

PREPARATION:

- Gather a few recipe books written for children, such as *The Spatulatta Cookbook* (Gerasole & Gerasole, 2007), which is written by the young Gerasole sisters and is an extension of their popular Web site where "Kids teach kids through video recipes." A number of other picture books that contain recipes are listed below.
- Select a simple recipe to prepare in front of the students.

Books That Contain Recipes	
Title and Author	**Recipe for . . .**
Chicks and Salsa (Reynolds, 2005)	Quackamole, Rooster's Roasted Salsa, and Hog Wild Nachos
The Giant Carrot (Peck, 1997)	Little Isabel's Carrot Puddin'
Little Red Riding Hood: A Newfangled Prairie Tale (Ernst, 1995)	Grandma's Wheat Berry Muffins
Stranger in the Woods (Sams & Stoick, 2000)	A snowman
Thunder Cake (Polacco, 1990)	Thunder Cake

EXPLANATION: A recipe is one way to introduce students to the informational genre of "how-to" writing. If recipes aren't of interest to you or your students, you could write a how-to book about riding a bike, building a snowman, or making a friend. For more information on instructional writing, refer to Tony Stead's book *Is That a Fact? Teaching Nonfiction Writing K–3* (2002).

DEMONSTRATION: As you go through the steps of making your selected recipe, record the following information:

- Name of food
- Number of servings
- Ingredients
- Directions

INVITATION: "Authors, you may want to think about your favorite food and write a recipe for that in your writer's notebook."

Part 3: Genre Exploration: Penning a Letter—From Postcards to Persuasion

EXPLANATION

In the genre exploration chart (page 112) you will find three ideas for letter-writing across the grades. (See Appendix A12, page 184, for postcard and letter-writing paper.) Of course, if your students' interests or your curriculum steers you in a different direction, you may want to explore an alternate real-world genre. If you've done some of the letter-writing mini-lessons contained in this chapter, then students have dabbled with letter-writing. The purpose of the genre exploration is to devote a week or so of the writing workshop to an in-depth study of a specific genre while students are engaged in writing a piece from that genre. For assessment purposes, writers' revised, polished work presents an opportunity for both student self-assessment and your own more formal assessment. Consider working with your students to create a rubric or checklist to guide both their assessment and yours. Most important, set aside some time to acknowledge students' growth and celebrate their efforts.

A postcard from the planet Mars

A letter to a future first grader

January Genre Exploration Chart Penning a Letter: From Postcards to Persuasion		
Kid-Friendly Definition of Genre: A *friendly letter* is written to a friend to share things about your life and to ask questions about his or hers. A *persuasive letter* is written to someone to try to convince or talk that person into doing or believing something.		
Characteristics of a Friendly Letter: • Written to a friend • Contains information about you • Poses questions about how your friend is doing • Includes a greeting, body, and closing		
Mentor Texts		
K	**1**	**2**
Postcards From Pluto: A Tour of the Solar System (Leedy, 1993). A sampling of brief postcards from the planets in the solar system	See page 107 for books containing friendly letters.	*Can I Have a Stegosaurus, Mom? Can I? Please!?* (Grambling, 1995) A boy uses both imaginative and practical reasons in his attempts to persuade his mother to get him a pet dinosaur.
Zooming In to Align Instruction Across the Grades		
K—Postcards	**1—Friendly Letter**	**2—Persuasive Letter**
A postcard includes: Greeting Brief body Closing Illustration	A friendly letter includes: Greeting Body Closing	See page 109 for a detailed mini-lesson.

Final Thoughts

Dear Reader,

We hope you and your students enjoyed learning about real-world genres. We can't wait to explore the genre of biography together! Isn't teaching writing a blast?

Best wishes,

Maria and Kathy

Chapter 6

February: Building an Understanding of Biographies

Another Holiday?

We always marvel at the number of holidays and other topics that one can pack into the shortest month of the year. Depending on your curriculum, you could be teaching about furry groundhogs and famous Americans such as Lincoln and Washington. In addition, time is spent sharing the interesting stories of notable figures in African American history, celebrating Valentine's Day, the 100th Day, and, depending on the year, Chinese New Year, too! Most likely, one focus of your social studies curriculum in February is the study of famous Americans; therefore, it is sensible to have students use the knowledge they gain from hearing a collection of biographies to write a biography of their own. With this goal in mind, we provide lessons here to immerse students in the inner workings of biographies.

Part 1: Morning Message Ideas and Samples

This month's messages will illuminate many of the structures and conventions found in biographical texts, such as chronological order and the capitalization of proper nouns. One of our students' favorite February messages involves the "Roses Are Red" poems (see below). We've enjoyed a lot of laughs and learning as we compose such poems with our young writers, and we hope you will, too!

MORNING MESSAGE IDEA: FEBRUARY WORD CHART

See explanation on page 35.

MORNING MESSAGE IDEA: ROSES ARE RED POEMS

If winter has left your students looking for fresh ideas, have a go at writing a few "Roses Are Red" poems together in the morning message. Soon your students will be penning their own unique poems. Not only will this message inspire ideas, but it also offers another occasion to practice rhyming words. To inspire young writers, read *Roses Are Pink, Your Feet Really Stink* (deGroat, 1996).

Morning Message Sample

February Word Chart

Valentine's Day	cards	Lincoln
president	candy	Washington
heart	groundhog	shadow
history	biography	famous

Morning Message Sample

Roses Are Red Poems

Roses are red.
Pickles are green.
Abraham Lincoln
was number sixteen.

Roses are red.
Daffodils are yellow.
General Washington
was a very brave
fellow.

In Ali's "Roses Are Red" poem he places quotation marks around each letter of "Let America Free." This overuse of punctuation is common when young writers first learn about particular marks.

MORNING MESSAGE IDEA: CAPITALIZING PROPER NOUNS 🔣 ✏️

To reinforce the convention of capitalizing proper nouns, write a message similar to the sample, and invite students to hunt for errors and edit your mistakes.

> **Morning Message Sample**
>
> ### Capitalizing Proper Nouns
>
> In the month of February, the students at brooks school will learn about ruby bridges, abraham lincoln, and groundhog day.

MORNING MESSAGE IDEA: THE LETTER STEALER—DIGRAPHS 🐛

See explanation on page 39.

> **Morning Message Sample**
>
> ### The Letter Stealer—Digraphs
>
> Abe liked to read and __ink in __e __ade of the __ite oak tree. (Abe liked to read and think in the shade of the white oak tree.)
>
> Wat__ out, George! Don't __op down __at __in __erry tree! (Watch out, George! Don't chop down that thin cherry tree!)

MORNING MESSAGE IDEA: WORD EXCHANGE ✴️

See explanation on page 37.

> ### Word Exchange
>
> Let's make a word exchange! What are other words that mean the same as LIKE?

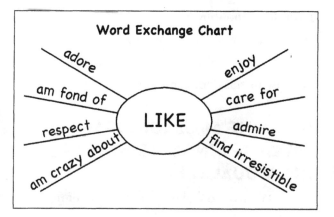

Word Exchange Chart

adore, am fond of, respect, am crazy about — LIKE — enjoy, care for, admire, find irresistible

MORNING MESSAGE IDEA: CHRONOLOGICAL ORDER 🌐

Authors often use chronological order to organize biographies and other texts; therefore, the concept of time order is an essential understanding for young writers.

> ## Morning Message Sample
>
> ### Chronological Order
>
> Can you put these sentences in chronological order?
>
> The groundhog saw his shadow.
> The groundhog ran back into his hole.
> The groundhog popped his head out of his hole.
>
> Abraham Lincoln was elected President.
> Abe grew up in a log cabin.
> Lincoln was a lawyer.
>
> I passed out my Valentine cards.
> I made my Valentine cards.
> I signed my Valentine cards.
>
> Washington was a general in the Revolutionary War.
> George Washington became our first President.
> When he was a boy, George loved to ride horses.

MORNING MESSAGE IDEA: FIRST- OR THIRD-PERSON VOICE

From read-alouds, teacher modeling, and studying mentor texts, your students have had numerous encounters with books written in either first- or third-person point of view. This message serves as a quick review or introduction to the terms first- and third-person point of view. To sneak in a little work on conventions, do not capitalize the word *I* so that children have to edit and discuss this error common to young writers.

> ## Morning Message Sample
>
> ### First- or Third-Person Voice
>
> Are the following sentences written in first- or third-person point of view?
>
> i can't wait until Valentine's Day!
> Francine wrote a note to Arthur.
> Do you think i will get any candy from my friends?
> Abe Lincoln loved to read books.

MORNING MESSAGE IDEA: INTERVIEWING INTERESTING INDIVIDUALS

Use this message to find out which current or historical public figure your students want to learn about and what questions they have for that person. This message will help uncover individual students' interests so that you can guide them in conducting their own investigation of a famous person via biographies or Internet-based research.

> ## Morning Message Sample
>
> ### Interviewing Interesting Individuals
>
> Day 1: If you could learn more about a famous person, who would you choose? Let's make a list!
>
> Day 2: What questions do you have for_____?

Read-Alouds for Writers		
Title and Author	**Brief Summary**	**Focus**
Abe Lincoln: The Boy Who Loved Books (Winters, 2003)	Winters's prose reads like poetry and spotlights Lincoln's love of learning. The biography ends, "He learned the power of words and used them well."	Sentence Fluency
Before John Was a Jazz Giant: A Song of John Coltrane (Weatherford, 2008)	Weatherford's repeated line, "Before John was a jazz giant . . .," hums along as readers listen to the sounds young Coltrane heard as he developed his style.	Sentence Fluency
Duke Ellington (Pinkney, 1998)	This jazzy book brings Duke and his music to life for young readers.	Word Choice
George Did It (Jurmain, 2006)	Readers might be surprised to find out that George Washington was reluctant to become our first President.	Ideas Voice
George Washington and the General's Dog (Murphy, 2002)	Murphy centers on Washington's love of animals in this "easy-reader" biography.	Ideas
How Ben Franklin Stole the Lightning (Schanzer, 2003)	In this lively biography, readers learn about the events leading up to Franklin's legendary kite experiment.	Voice
The Librarian of Basra: A True Story from Iraq (Winter, 2005)	The fascinating account of a librarian whose books "were more precious to her than mountains of gold."	Word Choice
Mr. Lincoln's Whiskers (Winnick, 1996)	A true story of 11-year-old Grace, who wrote to Mr. Lincoln advising him to grow a beard.	Ideas
Thank You, Sarah: The Woman Who Saved Thanksgiving (Anderson, 2002)	Return to this engaging Thanksgiving biography to discuss Anderson's unique approach to biographical writing.	Voice
The Story of Ruby Bridges (Coles, 1995)	A few quotations from Ruby's mother and teacher help tell the story of the sole African American girl to attend a court-ordered desegregated New Orleans school in 1960.	Word Choice

Part 2: A Menu of Mini-Lessons—Bringing Biographies to Life

After reading a biography, your students are sure to ask, "Is that person still alive? How old is she?" Certainly, the lives of famous people are fascinating. As you can see from the small sampling in the Read-Alouds for Writers chart (page 117), we are fortunate that children's book authors are writing more and more kid-friendly biographies. We now have a wealth of mentor texts from which to choose that not only teach about a diverse range of people but also use an array of writing techniques. As you sample and select books from this list or from your own collection, use a sticky note to jot down any particular pages or writing tips that you want to pinpoint in your read-aloud. After the mini-lesson, place the note inside the front cover of the book and you'll be ready when you reach for the book again next year! Let's begin bringing biographies to life.

MINI-LESSON: LEARNING LESSONS FROM THE PAST

PREPARATION:

- Select biographies of notable African Americans from different walks of life, such as Mae Jemison, Ruby Bridges, Duke Ellington, and George Washington Carver.
- Prepare a large chart similar to the one pictured below.
- Prepare individual booklets for students to record their own written responses.

EXPLANATION: The more individuals that students learn about, the more ideas they will have for their own writing. This lesson extends students' learning beyond reciting facts about the famous person to making connections between the individual's actions and choices and their own.

DEMONSTRATION: Read a biography. After reading, record the person's name, the title of the biography, the person's accomplishments, and a statement that summarizes what students have learned from that particular individual's life and accomplishments.

INVITATION: "Today I would like you to think about what you've learned from [title of biography] and record your response in your booklet."

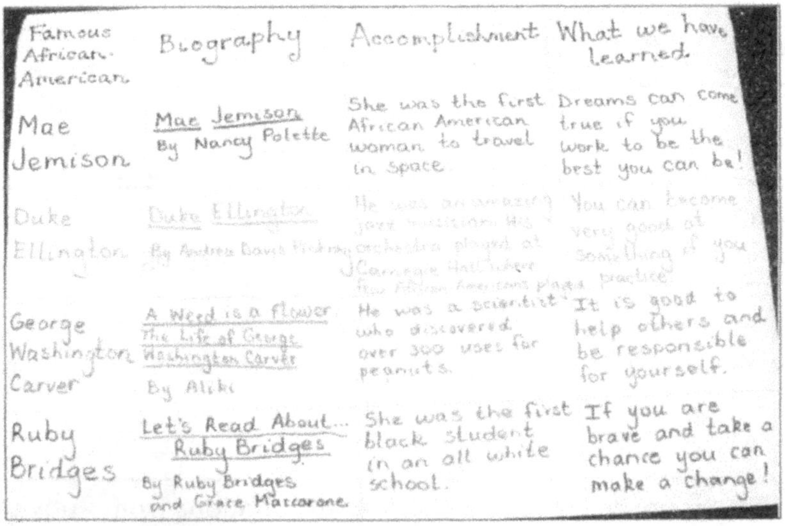

A chart helps students remember details and lessons about famous African Americans after reading and discussing biographies.

MINI-LESSON: NOTICING PROPER NOUNS 🌀

PREPARATION: Gather about 15–20 short biographies, such as Rookie Read-About Biographies (Scholastic), or a class set of student newspapers, such as *Scholastic News,* that include proper nouns in the text.

EXPLANATION: The aim of the mini-lesson is to raise students' awareness of proper nouns in the texts they are reading, and then to notice that writers use a capital letter at the beginning of a proper noun.

DEMONSTRATION: Introduce this mini-lesson by taking students on a "Proper-Noun Walk" around your school building. Look for the teachers' names above their doors, the name of the school out in front, and students' names on the work posted on bulletin boards. Once back in your room, ask students to work with a buddy to locate and record any proper nouns that they can find in a biography or student newspaper. Share and discuss their findings.

INVITATION: "Writers, as you reread your work, notice if you included any proper nouns in your writing. If so, bring them to share at the end of writing time."

MINI-LESSON: COMMON AND PROPER NOUNS 🌀

PREPARATION:

- Have a pocket chart on hand.
- Read and discuss *A Lime, a Mime, a Pool of Slime: More About Nouns* (Cleary, 2006). This book gives examples of the differences between common and proper nouns.
- Prepare a set of cards with both common and proper nouns related to a curricular area of study, and have a pocket chart handy to categorize the cards. The example at right is related to a study of famous African Americans.

EXPLANATION: Not only will this lesson help students differentiate between common and proper nouns, but it will also introduce or reinforce the vocabulary for a unit of study.

DEMONSTRATION: After reading, discuss the differences between common and proper nouns. Then, pass out noun cards and invite

Common and Proper Noun Cards

Duke Ellington	music	trumpet
Mae Jemison	space shuttle	doctor
Matthew Henson	explorer	North Pole
Ruby Bridges	student	school
George Washington Carver	peanut	plants

students to categorize them in the pocket chart as either common or proper nouns. Consider leaving the cards in the chart and adding to them as you learn more about prominent African Americans. As you model your own writing, use a sprinkling of proper nouns so that you can demonstrate the use of capital letters. For future practice with proper nouns, point them out as you read aloud.

INVITATION: "Authors, as you reread your work today, keep an eye out for proper nouns. When you write a proper noun, it should be capitalized. Reread and check to see if they are capitalized in your writing."

MINI-LESSON: TIME-ORDER ORGANIZATION

PREPARATION:

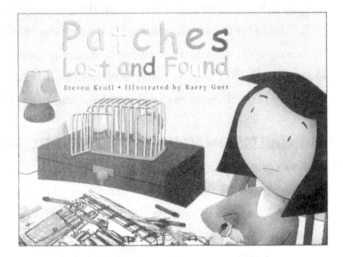

- Read and discuss a book about time-order organization, such as *Patches Lost and Found* (Kroll, 2001), in which a girl draws, and then writes, a story about losing and finding her pet guinea pig.
- Write a sequence of sentences on sentence strips or collect a series of pictures of an event. We learned a clever way to build a collection of sequencing pictures from Katie DeSotell, a seasoned reading teacher from Aurora, Illinois.

She taught us that if you have any worn-out picture books in your collection, instead of discarding them or giving them away, cut out a few key illustrations from the book, laminate the illustrations, and save them for sequencing lessons such as this one.

EXPLANATION: Numerous biographies are organized by chronology, or time order. In his picture-book biography series, David Adler uses chronological organization to give a historical account of each famous person.

DEMONSTRATION: Say, "Let's look back at the end of the book *Patches Lost and Found*. What do you notice about how Jenny organized her story?" Point out that she used a technique called storyboarding. Ask students if they have seen this technique described in the DVD extra features of a movie. Storyboarding is another way for children to chronologically organize their illustrations or words. If you are interested in learning more about using storyboards with your students, look for Roger Essley's book *Visual Tools for Differentiating Reading and Writing Instruction* (2008). Although the audience is teachers of grades 3–8, we've found a lot of ideas to implement in our classrooms.

INVITATION: "Today, writers, I would like you to draw a storyboard, or series of pictures, and then write a sentence or two about each picture."

MINI-LESSON: TRANSITION WORDS AND PHRASES

PREPARATION: Read aloud *Fluffy and Baron* (Rankin, 2006) or another text in which the author effectively uses transition words or phrases. In *Fluffy and Baron*, Baron, a farm dog, befriends a duckling named Fluffy. The story is based on the author's experiences with her own pets.

EXPLANATION: In Chapter 5 (see page 105), we featured a mini-lesson called "Yikes! I Have And-itis" that introduces the concept of connecting or transition words. Here we explore that concept in more depth, using a mentor text in which transition phrases are key to moving the plot along.

DEMONSTRATION: After reading for enjoyment, return to the text to write down the phrases the author used to move the story through time.

Transitional Phrases From *Fluffy and Baron*				
One summer day,	By autumn,	Four weeks later,	Everyday,	When it was time for dinner,
At night,	Then spring arrived,	After such a busy day,	As the summer passed,	For the next three nights,

INVITATION: "Authors use transition words and phrases to move their stories or their biographies through time. As you work today, notice if there is a place where you could add a transition word or phrase."

MINI-LESSON: CATEGORIZING FACTS ABOUT FAMOUS PEOPLE

PREPARATION:

- Preread a biography of your choice and select words or phrases that fit into four or more categories. (See chart, page 122.) For the example, we used Barbara Kerley's lively biography *What to Do About Alice?* (2008).
- Write words on sticky notes.
- Prepare chart with category headings.

EXPLANATION: This lesson serves two purposes. First, it introduces challenging vocabulary from the text. Then, it shows students how biographers organize their facts in various ways.

DEMONSTRATION: Prior to reading the biography, read the words/phrases to your students. As you read and discuss the meaning of the words and phrases, ask students to place them on the chart under the appropriate category. After reading, revisit the vocabulary to check if it has been placed in the correct cate-

Categorizing *What to Do About Alice?*	
People	**Places**
Theodore Roosevelt	Washington, D.C.
Alice Lee Roosevelt	White House
Congressman	Miss Spence's boarding
doctors	school
Personality	**Accomplishments**
read voraciously	became goodwill
wore leg braces	ambassador
was a tomboy	
drove a runabout	

gory. Don't miss the opportunity to go back into the text and notice that the author and illustrator use a variety of font styles and sizes and place many direct quotes in capitalized boldface print. These visual features help make this a lively biography.

INVITATION: "Authors, did you notice what techniques Barbara Kerley used not only to teach us about Alice but also to make us laugh at her antics? Think about how you could use the same techniques in your writing today." Discuss and orally rehearse some specific examples to jump-start students' writing.

MINI-LESSON: ABBREVIATIONS ?!

PREPARATION: Read a book with a lot of abbreviations; books about school with teachers' names work well.

EXPLANATION: Abbreviations can be found in many children's books, such as the Mr. Putter and Tabby series, and in the daily reading and writing that children do. This lesson teaches the conventions of abbreviations.

DEMONSTRATION: Say, "Writers, last month we learned about a famous man named Dr. Martin Luther King, Jr. [display his name in writing]. Do you notice anything interesting about his name?" Once a child notices the abbreviations in his name, discuss what they stand for and how they are punctuated. Ask students if they are familiar with any other abbreviations and make a reference chart.

Dr.	doctor
St.	street
Jr.	junior
Mrs.	mistress
Mr.	mister

INVITATION: "Writers, note that when you are writing about a teacher at our school, such as Mr. Hatch or Mrs. Pipkin, you place a period after the abbreviation."

MINI-LESSON: USING THE WORD WALL TO SPELL HIGH-FREQUENCY WORDS

PREPARATION: To teach this lesson, you will need a collection of high-frequency words posted on a classroom word wall. If you are interested in more information on teaching and practicing high-frequency words in the word wall format, look for these books:

Month-by-Month Phonics for First Grade (Cunningham & Hall, 2002)

Month-by-Month Phonics for Second Grade (Hall & Cunningham, 2001)

Phonics They Use: Words for Reading and Writing (Cunningham, 2009)

EXPLANATION: If you expect your students to spell high-frequency words correctly, then it is essential that you teach, practice, and model the use of the word wall on a regular basis. We included this lesson in this chapter as a gentle reminder, in case your teaching of high-frequency words has taken a back seat to other important lessons.

DEMONSTRATION: As you are modeling your writing, be sure to point out how you locate and use words from the word wall.

INVITATION: "Editors, today I would like you to orally reread your work from yesterday, keeping an eye out for spelling. Check to see that any word wall words are spelled correctly."

A first-grade word wall

MINI-LESSON: WHAT ARE MY INITIALS?

PREPARATION: Read and discuss either *A. Lincoln and Me* (Borden, 2000) or *My Brother Martin* (King, 2003). In both biographies the authors use the person's initials when talking about him.

EXPLANATION: You might be surprised to discover how few children actually know their initials. This lesson will familiarize students with their own initials and with the fact that many people—including authors such as J. K. Rowling and E. B. White—use initials rather than their names.

DEMONSTRATION: After reading one of the biographies listed above, discuss the use of the person's initials. Ask students to turn to a neighbor and say their own initials. Then prompt students, "Next time you are reading, look for authors' initials on the covers of books and point them out when you find them."

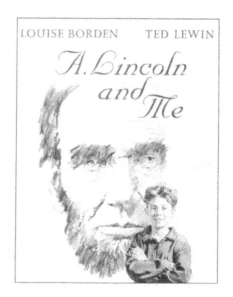

INVITATION: "Today, writers, I will dismiss you by saying your initials. When you hear your initials, you may gather your writing materials and find your perfect writing spot."

Part 3: Genre Exploration: Writing a Biography— Future Famous Americans 🔊

EXPLANATION

With all the biographical knowledge students have gained during writing time, they are well prepared to pen a biography or, in kindergarten, an illustrated timeline. For this particular genre exploration, along with the genre exploration chart, we've included the day-by-day plan we followed for doing "biography buddies." As you can see from the student's journal entry at right, the excitement surrounding this genre exploration was high! Students enjoyed having the opportunity to learn more and write about their friends.

The students were excited about writing a biography.

A DAY-BY-DAY PLAN FOR BIOGRAPHY BUDDIES

PREPARATION:

- Read aloud engaging biographies such as those listed in the Read-Alouds for Writers section.
- Pair students with a "biography buddy."
- Make one copy of My Interview Notebook for each student by stapling the pages together across the top to form a handy booklet. See Appendix A13, pages 185–186.
- Conduct your own interview with a family member, friend, or colleague, using the interview notebook.

Mini-Lesson 1:

- Brainstorm interview questions in the following four categories: Family, Friends, Favorites, Fun Facts

Mini-Lesson 2:

- Show students the Interview Notebook pages. Explain that you left blank spaces to add additional questions from the chart they created in Mini-Lesson 1.
- Tell students that they will begin interviewing their biography buddies by asking them questions about their families from the first page of their interview notebooks.

February Genre Exploration Chart Writing a Biography: Future Famous Americans

Kid-Friendly Definition of Genre: A biography is a piece of writing that tells facts and interesting details about a real person.

Characteristics of Genre:
- Written in third person
- Tells about a real person
- Describes the person's life, actions, and relationships with others
- Includes interesting, sometimes lesser-known details about the person

Mentor Texts

K	1	2
Create an illustration of an event from your life to share with your students.	See Read-Alouds for Writers on page 117.	See Read-Alouds for Writers on page 117.

Zooming In to Align Instruction Across the Grades

K—Illustrated Timeline	1—Biography Buddies	2—Interesting Individuals

• Send a note home requesting that parents help their child to draw or write some information about the four events listed below.
• Using the information, write or draw an illustrated timeline about each category.
  — The Day I Was Born
  — Before I Started K
  — The First Day of K
  — Today
• Revise, polish, and present.
	See A Day-By-Day Plan for Biography Buddies, starting on page 124.	• Select a subject for biography, such as a family member, cross-age buddy, or a member of the school faculty or staff.
		• Compose a list of questions.
		• Interview the person and record answers to questions.
		• Use the answers to write a biography.
		• Revise, edit, polish, and present.

- Model interviewing one of your students about his or her family while the rest of the class observes fishbowl style (you and the student in the middle of circle, the rest of the class sitting in a circle observing).

- Discuss interviewing tips:
  - Be a great listener!
  - Take turns asking questions. (Having pairs of students do "tag team" interviewing—Student A asks Student B a question and records the answer, and then the two reverse roles—reduces the amount of writing that one child does at a time and cuts down on fatigue from extended writing.)
  - Don't interrupt.
  - If you have trouble writing down your buddy's answer, ask him or her to repeat it.
  - Be enthusiastic and positive, and say thank you when you are finished (Robb, 2004).
- Assign buddies and send students to interview.
- When they're finished with the interviews, invite each student to share one interesting tidbit they learned about their buddy's family.

Students interview each other using their interview notebook.

Students share their finished biographies.

Mini-Lessons 3–5:

Follow the same format as in Mini-Lesson 2 for conducting interviews about their buddy's friends, favorites, and fun facts. Each mini-lesson addresses just one interview topic.

Mini-Lessons 4–7:

Using your own interview notebook, model how to take the answers from the questions and turn them into sentences. Return to mentor texts to point out interesting leads and unique writing techniques.

Mini-Lessons 8–10:

Revise, polish, and celebrate!

Final Thoughts

February flew by in its usual fun- and fact-filled fashion. Students have listened to, read, studied, and penned their own biographies. Along the way, they have learned some lessons about notable historical figures and about ways they can apply those lessons to their own lives. As always, it was another productive month in the primary grades.

Chapter 7

March: Peeking Into Poetry

The Sights and Sounds of Spring

Because we live in the Midwest, the first signs of spring bring renewed energy (sometimes too much!) to our winter-weary students. As they play and explore, children delight in the sights and sounds of the outdoor world. Therefore, we capitalize on their enthusiasm by teaching students how to capture their experiences in poetic ways. We realize that poetry month typically occurs in April. However, if your teaching life is anything like ours, you probably find that the plans from one month spill into the next. If you begin now, by the time April arrives, your students will be seasoned poets. The main goal of this chapter is to help you immerse students in the genre of poetry. Children are more likely to become poets if they have plenty of time to sample, savor, and discover the joys of well-written poems. Along with exploring the realm of poetry, you can gently guide students to try their hand at writing poems of their own. In addition, build children's poetry know-how by providing frequent occasions for them to notice and name the elements of poetry, such as rhythm and rhyme, sound patterns, shape, figurative language, and the other imaginative ways poets play with ideas and words.

Part 1: Morning Message Ideas and Samples

For the messages this month, gather a collection of short poems. We've included some of our favorite poetry books in the Read-Alouds for Writers section on page 133, but we are certain you have your own. In many instances, you can use our message idea with your favorite poem.

MORNING MESSAGE IDEA: THE CONVENTIONS OF POETRY ?!

This month you can transform the morning message into a morning poem to introduce different types of poetry. In preparation, write a poem on the chalkboard, chart paper, sentence strips, or an overhead transparency, or project it using a document camera. Each day, introduce a poem and its author. Next, read it aloud to savor the language. To boost reading fluency, follow the read-aloud with a choral reading. Conclude by returning to the poem to notice the poet's choice of language and elements. For a lively poem to kick off your poetry unit, choose Brod Bagert's poem "Shout" from his book *Shout! Little Poems That Roar* (2007).

MORNING MESSAGE IDEA: MARCH WORD CHART

See explanation on page 35.

Morning Message Sample

March Word Chart

St. Patrick's Day	leprechaun	rainbow
spring	shamrock	green
lucky	windy	kite
lion	lamb	weather

MORNING MESSAGE IDEA: THE LETTER STEALER—BLENDS

See explanation on page 39.

Morning Message Sample

The Letter Stealer—Blends

Today for a __ecial __eat we'll eat some __een cookies.
(Today for a special treat we'll eat some green cookies.)

MORNING MESSAGE IDEA: WORD EXCHANGE

See explanation on page 37.

Morning Message Sample

Word Exchange

Let's make a word exchange! What are other words that mean the same as BRIGHT?

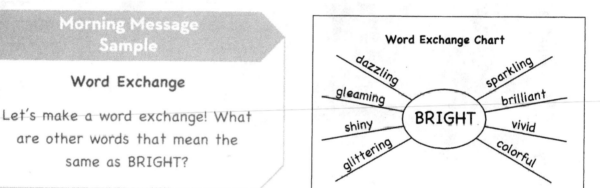

Word Exchange Chart

dazzling
gleaming
shiny
glittering

BRIGHT

sparkling
brilliant
vivid
colorful

MORNING MESSAGE IDEA: THE LEPRECHAUNS WERE HERE!

Imagine your students' delight when they discover that the leprechauns visited their classroom and messed up the morning message!

Morning Message Sample

The Leprechauns Were Here!

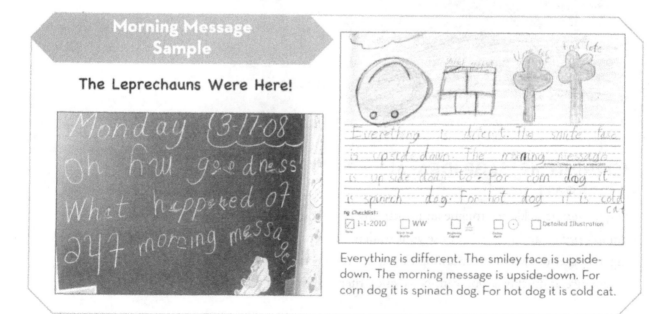

Everything is different. The smiley face is upside-down. The morning message is upside-down. For corn dog it is spinach dog. For hot dog it is cold cat.

MORNING MESSAGE IDEA: PIGGYBACK SONGS

Piggyback songs offer an accessible way for children to compose songs of their very own. We use familiar tunes such as "Frère Jacques," "The Farmer in the Dell," "Happy Birthday to You," and "Camptown Races" to write songs based on the color songs, such as *Sing and Read "Red,"* available in the Color Word books from Frog Street Press.

Morning Message Sample

Piggyback Songs

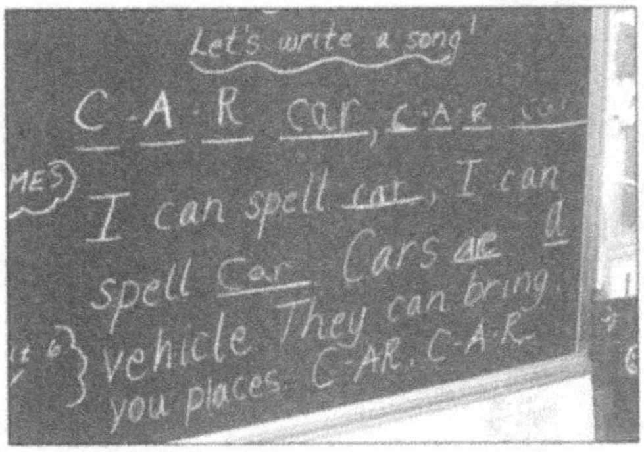

Sing to the tune of "Frère Jacques."

Sing to the tune of "Camptown Races."

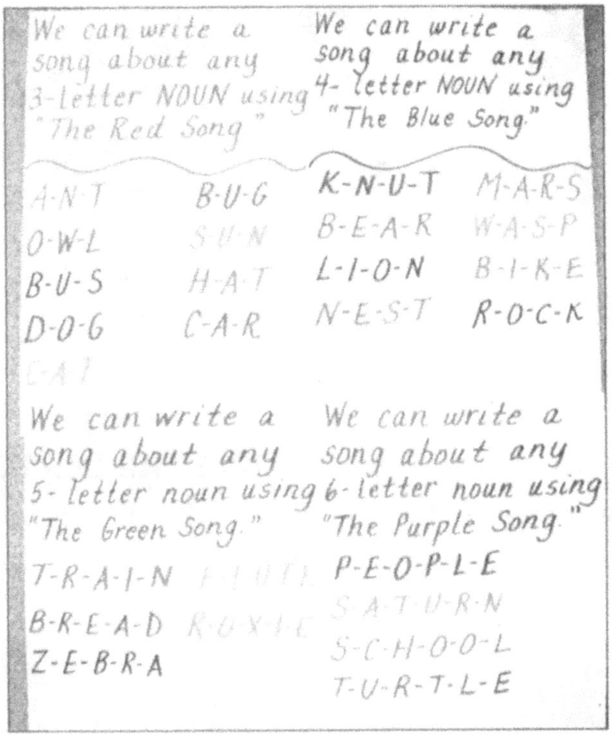

"Color Song Ideas" chart

MORNING MESSAGE IDEA: ALL ABOUT ALLITERATION

Tongue twisters tickle the tongue and teach tiny tots about the term *alliteration* and its uses! Amuse your students by writing a tongue twister or two in the morning message. Chorally read the sentence as quickly as you can. Next, ask writers to join

Morning Message Sample

All About Alliteration

Lucky the Leprechaun lived on Lemon Lane.

you in a word-play challenge by creating their own tongue twister. Add the book of easy-to-read tongue twisters, *Busy Buzzing Bumblebees* (Schwartz, 1992), to your collection of poetry books.

MORNING MESSAGE IDEA: POETS WRITE ABOUT THINGS THEY LOVE

Poets write about subjects that are near to their hearts. Use a morning message early in the month to create a chart of students' treasured topics. As the month continues, students can refer to this list when they choose topics for their poetry writing.

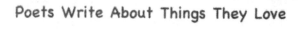

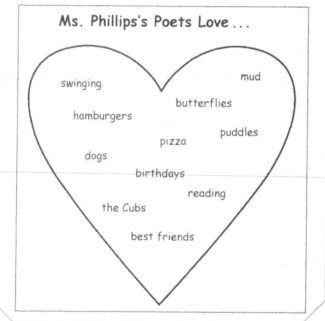

MORNING MESSAGE IDEA: RHYME TIME

It is important for students to understand that not every poem has to rhyme. If students choose to create poems that rhyme, it is helpful to give them resources and strategies for generating rhyming words. A clever way to begin a rhyming message is with Douglas Florian's "Do-It-Yourself Poem" found on page 122 of *Laugh-eteria* (1999). Another option is to write the beginning of a nursery rhyme, and then ask students to supply new alternatives to the original rhyme.

Morning Message Sample

Rhyme Time

Little Bo Peep
lost her _____. (sleep, jeep, beep)

Old King Cole
was a merry old _____.
(troll, foal, bowl, mole)

MORNING MESSAGE IDEA: VIVID VERBS 🖐

Vivid verbs add motion to poems and rhymes. If needed, revisit some of the books in Chapter 3 that introduce the concept of verbs. For this message, write a sentence with an ordinary verb and then invite students to share a more vivid verb to move the sentence along.

> **Morning Message Sample**
>
> **Vivid Verbs**
>
> **Can you replace the verb in this sentence?**
> The snake went through the grass.

MORNING MESSAGE IDEA: AMAZING ADJECTIVES 🖐

Once you've had an opportunity to confer with students and jot down some common topics, use this message to explore adjective alternatives that describe the students' chosen topics. You may want to reread some of the adjective concept books found in Chapter 4. Mary O'Neill's poem "Feelings About Words" is the ideal poem to kick off this lesson. It appears on page 197 of *The Random House Book of Poetry for Children* (Prelutsky, 1983). To prepare the message, simply write a topic in the middle of a word web and record the adjectives on the lines as pictured in the sample at right.

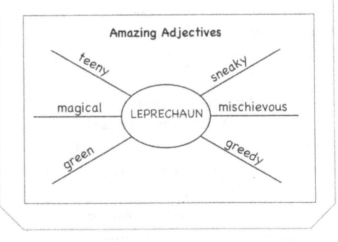

> **Morning Message Sample**
>
> **Amazing Adjectives**
>
> Poets, what adjective would you use to describe [the sun, the stars, a leprechaun, a flower, a thunderstorm, and so on]?
>
> **Amazing Adjectives**
>
> teeny sneaky
> magical LEPRECHAUN mischievous
> green greedy

Read-Alouds for Writers	
Title and Author	**Brief Summary**
Here's a Little Poem: A Very First Book of Poetry (Yolen & Peters, 2007)	A must-have collection for kindergarten poets, with 61 large-print, brightly illustrated poems
The New Kid on the Block (Prelutsky, 1984)	This is the first of Prelutsky's humorous, kid-favorite anthologies illustrated by James Stevenson. The poetry and laughter continue in *Something Big Has Been Here* (1990), *A Pizza the Size of the Sun* (1996), *It's Raining Pigs & Noodles* (2000), and *My Dog May Be a Genius* (2008).
The Random House Book of Poetry for Children (Prelutsky, 1983)	A comprehensive collection of 572 poems, with illustrations by Arnold Lobel
Riddle-icious (Lewis, 1996)	Lewis's lively, rhyming, poetic riddles will keep students guessing.
Sing a Song of Popcorn (de Regniers, Moore, White, & Carr, 1988)	A collection of 115 poems illustrated by nine Caldecott-winning artists
Where the Sidewalk Ends (Silverstein, 1974)	Silverstein's beloved collection of poems and pictures; also, sample poems from *A Light in the Attic* (1981)

Part 2: A Menu of Mini-Lessons—Discovering Poetry Possibilities

When it comes to poetry, the possibilities are endless. For our youngest writers, we begin by teaching them the elements of poetry rather than the various types of poems, such as acrostic, haiku, and so on. If you are looking for books and teaching ideas about specific types of poems, see Chapter 8 in *Literature Is Back!* (Fuhler & Walther, 2007). To generate interest and enthusiasm for this month's writing mini-lessons, set up a poetry corner—or basket, if your classroom space is limited like ours—and stock it with a sampling of poetry books. You may also include laminated photos or calendar pictures of possible poetry topics. Once you've done this, you're ready to explore the sights and sounds cleverly created by poets.

MINI-LESSON: POETS WRITE ABOUT THINGS THEY LOVE 〇 〇

PREPARATION: Select a picture book or poem about poetry—here are two possibilities:

- *There Is a Flower at the Tip of My Nose Smelling Me* (Walker, 2006)

- "Finding a Poem" by Karla Kuskin, in *Wonderful Words* (Hopkins, 2004)

EXPLANATION: The more young writers know about a topic, the easier it will be for them to create an idea-filled poem.

DEMONSTRATION: Say, "I'm going to begin by thinking about a few topics for my poems, things I know a lot about and love. Let's see, I might write a poem about _____." Demonstrate listing a few potential poetry topics. "To prepare for writing a poem, I will choose a topic and make a quick list of descriptive words or phrases related to that topic." Brainstorm words and phrases, or draw illustrations. This is a good stopping point for one day. The next day, reread and revise your ideas. Continue by saying, "Once I have a page filled with words, I begin playing with them to create a poem."

INVITATION: "Poets, before you begin writing today, think about things that you love. What would you like to write a poem about this month? Consider starting a list of poetry possibilities."

MINI-LESSON: POETS WRITE ABOUT THINGS THEY KNOW— EXPLORING SCHOOL AND ANIMAL POEMS

PREPARATION: Prior to this mini-lesson, collect a few poetry anthologies organized around topics that are familiar to your students, such as school and animals. You may decide to select poems related to a unit of study or those favored by your young poets.

School Poems	Animal Poems
Hello School! (Lillegard, 2001)	*Bow Wow Meow Meow* (Florian, 2003)
Mrs. Cole on an Onion Roll (Dakos, 1995)	*A Pet for Me* (Hopkins, 2003)
School Supplies: A Book of Poems (Hopkins, 1996)	*Sea Stars: Saltwater Poems* (Harley, 2006)

EXPLANATION: Young writers are most successful when writing poems about familiar topics. By reading a sampling of poems from a few themed poetry titles, budding poets will notice similarities and differences among the poems. Likewise, they will gather techniques that they can apply to their own poetry writing.

DEMONSTRATION: Say, "After reading all of those poems about school, let's make a chart titled 'Here's What We Noticed About the School Poems.'" Here are some possible "noticings" that students will offer:

- The poets wrote about things such as swings, scissors, paper clips, and lunchbags.
- Some poems rhymed, while others did not rhyme.
- Some poems were only two lines long; others were much longer.
- Kalli Dakos used onomatopoeia in "The Bumbling Day."
- Our favorite poems were _____ because . . .

Continue, "Using what I've learned from reading all of these books, I think I'm ready to try writing a school poem of my own. Let's see, I think I'll write about _____." Continue the process of drafting your own poem, as you did in the previous mini-lesson, Poets Write About Things They Love, on pages 133–134.

INVITATION: "Poets, are you ready to give it a try? Today you may continue a poem you were working on or choose to write your own school poem."

MINI-LESSON: POETS USE SOUND PATTERNS—ALLITERATION

PREPARATION: Collect books or poems with alliterative language such as:

- *A My Name Is Alice* (Bayer, 1984)
- "Batty" found in *Laugh-eteria* (Florian, 1999)
- *Four Famished Foxes and Fosdyke* (Edwards, 1995)

EXPLANATION: Alliteration is the repetition of the beginning consonant. Listening for and identifying alliteration not only boosts young writers' phonemic awareness, but also offers a handy technique to incorporate in their own writing.

DEMONSTRATION: Work in a shared writing format to compose a poem or a few tongue twisters to demonstrate the use of alliteration.

INVITATION: "As you reread your poem aloud, listen carefully to the words. Can you replace a word or two to make an alliterative line?"

MINI-LESSON: POETS USE SOUND WORDS—ONOMATOPOEIA

PREPARATION: Picture book authors frequently sprinkle sound words throughout their texts. As you are reading such texts, point out these words or collect them on a chart or separate word cards.

Books With Onomatopoeia	
Achoo! Bang! Crash! The Noisy Alphabet (MacDonald, 2003)	An alphabet book filled with onomatopoeic words
Phooey! (Rosenthal, 2007)	Reach for this book when you want an adventure that features onomatopoeia.
Slop Goes the Soup (Edwards, 2001)	A clumsy warthog's sneeze begins an onomatopoeic chain of events.

Poems With Onomatopoeia	
Poem	**Appears in . . .**
"Ears Hear" by Lucia and James L. Hymes, Jr. (p. 8)	*Poems Go Clang!* (Gliori, 1997)
"The Fourth" (p. 15)	*Where the Sidewalk Ends* (Silverstein, 1974)
"Push Button" (p. 158)	*A Light in the Attic* (Silverstein, 1981)
"Weather" by Eve Merriam (p. 15)	*Sing a Song of Popcorn* (de Regniers et al., 1988)

EXPLANATION: One technique that some poets use is onomatopoeia. Words that sound like the noise they describe are appealing to young writers.

DEMONSTRATION: Say, "Wow! Did you notice all the sound words in that book/poem? Can you remember what some of them were? Let's begin a collection of sound words on this chart. I think I will go back to the poem I was working on yesterday and add a sound word or two."

INVITATION: "Poets, you can start your own onomatopoeia collection in your writing folder or look for a place in a poem where you can spice it up by adding onomatopoeia."

Yesterday Dr. Walther taught us what an onomatopoeia is. It is something that is a sound effect.

MINI-LESSON: POETS USE RHYTHM—REPEATED LINES

PREPARATION: Gather picture books or poems in which the author uses a repeated line or lines. Before you begin reading, ask students to listen carefully to see if they can detect a poetic technique that adds rhythm. Read the poem or the book aloud to your students and discuss the use of repeated lines.

Picture Books Featuring Repeated Lines		
I Love Our Earth (Martin & Sampson, 2006)		The beauty of nature is celebrated in this lyrical text with the repeated line "I love our Earth."
Where I Live (Wolfe, 2001)		Visit the seaside as the young narrator describes the details of her home.
The Wolves Are Back (George, 2008)		Learn about the elimination and return of the wolves to Yellowstone National Park.

Poems Featuring Repeated Lines	
Poem	**Appears in . . .**
"Here Comes Summer" (p. 33)	*A Light in the Attic* (Silverstein, 1981)
"Today's a Foggy Foggy Day" (p. 36)	*A Pizza the Size of the Sun* (Prelutsky, 1996; note: Many poems in this collection have repeated lines.)

EXPLANATION: You can find many poetry techniques in the picture books in your classroom. During a read-aloud, a quick pause to highlight a technique such as a repeated line raises students' awareness and provides a mentor text for future writing. Consider placing picture books that use similar techniques together in a basket or on a bookshelf for easy access during writing workshop.

DEMONSTRATION: Model using a repeated line to begin composing a poem about a topic of your choice. You might be thinking, "I can't write a poem with a repeated line." But remember, it is important for students to watch you mess about as you try to create a poem. Experiment with different words, cross out those that don't work, use the thesaurus to look for others. If you think of a better way to say something, change your poem. This is the real work of a writer. A polished poem is rarely written in the first draft.

INVITATION: "Poets, you may want to play with the technique of a repeated line in your poem. To do this, choose an important idea or line in a poem you've already written and experiment with repeating it a number of times throughout the poem."

MINI-LESSON: POETS USE RHYME 🎵

PREPARATION:
- Select a number of poems with rhyme.
- Locate a rhyming dictionary, such as *The Scholastic Rhyming Dictionary* (Young, 1997).

EXPLANATION: Rhyme is a prevalent element in poems for children. Before students can add this element to their own poetry, we must ensure they have a firm grasp of rhyme. To instill this understanding, provide repeated readings of rhyming books and poems and give children lots of practice generating word-family lists during Words for Writers lessons (see page 64 for a sample lesson). This exposure will help your writers become more proficient at listening for, identifying, and supplying rhymes for specific words.

DEMONSTRATION: After spending a few days studying rhyming poems, work with the students in a shared writing format to compose a rhyming poem.

INVITATION: "Poets, we've worked hard together to write a poem that has rhyming words. If you're up for the challenge of writing one of your own, give it a try. I'll be here to lend a helping hand."

MINI-LESSON: POETS USE SHAPE—CONCRETE POEMS 🌐

PREPARATION: Gather books that contain concrete poems, such as *Come to My Party and Other Shape Poems* (Roemer, 2004).

EXPLANATION: In a concrete poem, the poet writes the words in such a way that they appear to be the object described. For the youngest writers, it is helpful if you select poems about familiar topics to read aloud as mentor poems.

DEMONSTRATION: This demonstration will take a few days to complete. As you demonstrate each step, invite learners to do the same in their writer's notebook.

- Select a topic that can be represented by an object. Brainstorm a list of words or phrases that describe the topic.
- Put the words together in a poem.
- Reread, revise, edit, and polish the poem.
- Draw a pencil outline of the shape of the topic/object. Write the words along the edge of the pencil line. One snag that children encounter is having too many or too few words to match their outline. Possible solutions to this dilemma include repeating a line or adding details to the shape to accommodate extra words.
- Erase the pencil line. Add color with colored pencils.
- Celebrate and share.

INVITATION: "Poets, we're going to work side by side for a few days to create shape poems. Let's get started!"

MINI-LESSON: POETS USE VIVID VERBS 🖐

PREPARATION:

- To introduce this lesson, read Jack Prelutsky's poem "Alphabet Stew," found on page 188 of *The Random House Book of Poetry for Children* (Prelutsky, 1983).

- Select a poem or two to highlight the use of verbs. Reproduce the poem on an overhead or use a document camera to project the poem so that students can see the words. Here are some poems that work well:

  - "Last Night I Dreamed of Chickens" from *Something Big Has Been Here* (Prelutsky, 1990) includes the verbs *pecking, ruffling, roosting,* and *clucking.*

  - Karla Kuskin's poem "Spring," found in *The Random House Book of Poetry for Children* (Prelutsky, 1983), uses verbs such as *swinging* and *buzzing* to illuminate the joys of spring.

  - "When Tillie Ate the Chili" appears in *The New Kid on the Block* (Prelutsky, 1984) and features such verbs as *erupted, fled,* and *sputtered.*

EXPLANATION: Take advantage of the vivid verbs found in poetry to review and reinforce the concept of verbs.

DEMONSTRATION: Read the poems aloud. Afterwards, invite students to join in a choral reading of the poems. Discuss the poet's use of verbs. Brainstorm alternatives.

INVITATION: "Poets, can you reread one of the poems you have written and revise it to include more vivid verbs? If you do that today, mark it with a sticky note and bring it over when we share."

MINI-LESSON: POETS USE SENSORY IMAGES 🖐

PREPARATION: Review with students the work you did with settings and senses in Chapter 4. Then select poems that illuminate the use of sensory images, such as those found in the chart below.

Poems With Sensory Images		
Sense	**Poem**	**Appears in . . .**
Sight	"I Made Something Strange With My Chemistry Set" (p. 58)	*A Pizza the Size of the Sun* (Prelutsky, 1996)
Sound	"Louder Than a Clap of Thunder" (p. 36)	*The New Kid on the Block* (Prelutsky, 1984)
Taste	"Crunch and Lick" by Dorothy Aldis (p. 67)	*Read-Aloud Rhymes for the Very Young* (Prelutsky, 1986)
Touch	"No Matter" (p. 18)	*Good Rhymes, Good Times* (Hopkins, 1995)
Smell	"Smells" by Kathryn Worth (p. 39)	*The Random House Book of Poetry for Children* (Prelutsky, 1983)

EXPLANATION: Exploring the concept of sensory images in poetry is directly related to the reading comprehension strategy of visualizing or making mental images.

DEMONSTRATION: As you read a selected poem, ask students to identify the sense or senses the writer is using to help create a vivid image. Ask listeners to sketch the images they see, hear, taste, touch, or smell. Record any words or phrases that contain sensory images students might include in their own poems. In your demonstration, reread your own poems to find a place where you could strengthen your writing by including a sensory image.

INVITATION: "Poets work hard to use words that paint pictures so that readers can visualize what the poem is describing. Read your poem to a friend and ask if he or she can make a mental picture as you read your words."

MINI-LESSON: POETS USE CREATIVE CONVENTIONS 🔲

PREPARATION: Collect poems that contain creative conventions. Enlarge selected poems by making an overhead transparency or displaying the poem using a document camera.

Poems That Use Creative Conventions		
Poem	**Appears in . . .**	**Creative Convention**
"The Dalmatian" (p. 21)	*Bow Wow Meow Meow* (Florian, 2003)	Each letter **o** in the poem is filled in to look like a dot.
"Good Books, Good Times" (p. 17)	*Good Books, Good Times* (Hopkins, 1990)	The lines are two-word sentences.
"I'm All Mixed Up" (p. 106)	*A Pizza the Size of the Sun* (Prelutsky, 1996)	The text alternates between lowercase and capital letters to give a mixed-up appearance.
"Lazy Jane" (p. 87)	*Where the Sidewalk Ends* (Silverstein, 1974)	Each line has only one word.
"The Polliwogs" (p. 30)	*Lizards, Frogs, and Polliwogs* (Florian, 2001)	The word *polliwog* and all the verbs are set to look as if they are moving.

EXPLANATION: Poets use conventions to convey meaning, to add a distinct rhythm, or to evoke a visual image. The more samples of creative conventions you can find, the more options students will have as they pen their own poems.

DEMONSTRATION: Display a poem with creative conventions. Read the poem aloud, and then invite learners to join in for a choral reading. Discuss and record the unique conventions found in the poem. As you continue studying conventions found in different poems, invite students to record ideas in their writer's notebooks or post the poems on a bulletin board for future reference.

INVITATION: "Poets, let your poem and your imagination be your guide as you decide what kinds of conventions you might want to use."

Part 3: Genre Exploration: Composing Poetry— Playing With Words

EXPLANATION

The upbeat tempo of poetry has permeated this month's read-alouds, morning messages, and mini-lessons. Many of the poems you studied this month appear in poetry collections or anthologies. For the genre exploration, students will compile their own collection of poems. (See March Genre Exploration Chart on the next page.) For kindergarten students, this may be a poem or two; with older children the number of poems will be greater. During the writing workshop, students may have already penned a number of poems in their writer's notebook. Certainly, they can finish, revise, and polish their works in progress and then add a few fresh poems to their collection. To celebrate the completion of this genre exploration, invite students to share their poetry with another class or invite family members for an afternoon poetry party.

Final Thoughts

Toes are tapping, fingers snapping,
Playful language fills the air.
Long poems, short poems, tall poems, small poems—
Children write, then polish and share.

Surround them with the words of poets,
Read and chant and think and write.
Poems that wiggle, poems that giggle—
Soon their poems will be out of sight!

March Genre Exploration Chart
Composing Poetry: Playing With Words

Kid-Friendly Definition of Genre: A poem is a special way to write about a topic using a small number of powerful words. The ideas for poetry come from your life or from your imagination.

Characteristics of Genre:
- Plays with the sounds of words and the rhythmic language patterns
- Uses vivid language to create sensory images
- Condenses ideas into a shorter format than prose
- Presented in various shapes, sizes, and forms

Mentor Texts

K	1	2
See Read-Alouds for Writers chart on page 133.	*Read a Rhyme, Write a Rhyme* (Prelutsky, 2005). This picture book is organized by topics such as bugs, friends, birthdays, and rain, and offers a sampling of poems on each subject, with a "poemstart" to fuel the imagination. This would be a helpful resource for your reluctant poets.	*Outside the Lines: Poetry at Play* (Burg, 2002). A playful collection of shape poems all about the games children play *Pizza, Pigs, and Poetry: How to Write a Poem* (Prelutsky, 2008). Children's Poet Laureate Jack Prelutsky offers children 20 writing tips, such as how to turn their own experiences into poems and how to write a concrete poem.

Zooming In to Align Instruction Across the Grades

K—A Poetry Collection	1—A Poetry Collection	2—A Poetry Collection
Create a number of poems in a shared or interactive writing format. Type the poems and give them to students to illustrate.	Consider challenging your students to include one rhyming poem.	Consider challenging your students to include a concrete poem in their collection.

Chapter 8

April & May: Navigating Nonfiction

End With a Bang, a Collection of Bugs, or a Cute Polar Bear!

Most likely, you can name a handful of students who astonish you with their recall of fascinating facts about dinosaurs, insects, presidents, or another subject on which they have checked out every book in the library. Fact finders will pour over nonfiction texts to discover the inner workings of a volcano or the details of the *Titanic*'s sinking. As you would with any in-depth study, immerse students in the genre of nonfiction by collecting, reading, and discussing nonfiction texts about a wide range of topics. To make it more convenient for students to consult mentor texts as they craft their own nonfiction pieces, allot separate shelves or baskets for nonfiction titles. Along with tips for writing factual pieces, the messages and mini-lessons in this chapter acquaint students with the distinctive features or conventions of nonfiction texts such as captions, labels, maps, and charts.

House nonfiction books on a separate shelf.

Part 1: Morning Message Ideas and Samples

Although this chapter covers the last couple of months of the school year, we are adding only a handful of new non-fiction-focused messages to your collection. In addition to revisiting the messages from previous chapters, you can now provide an opportunity for your students to take the lead. After spending the year writing messages with your students, put them in charge by allowing them to become the "Writer of the Day" (see page 148). Over the years, we've gathered a lot of new ideas as we watch students generate their own messages. If you choose to do this, have a digital camera handy to record their clever morning message ideas!

MORNING MESSAGE IDEA: APRIL AND MAY WORD CHARTS

See explanation on page 35.

Morning Message Sample

April Word Chart

April Fool's Day	baseball	Earth Day
umbrella	recycle	rainy
cloudy	rainforest	pollution
endangered animals	thunderstorm	environment

Cubs and Sox (or your students' favorite teams)

Morning Message Sample

May Word Chart

flowers	swimming	sprinkler	frogs
Mother's Day	bugs	picnics	Memorial Day
parades	butterflies	ice cream	vacation

MORNING MESSAGE IDEA: NONFICTION! 🔦

To learn more about your students' areas of expertise prior to immersing them in nonfiction texts, query your class to discover their shared interests. The information you gather will help guide your selection of resources. Moreover, young writers will know which "class expert" to consult when they have a question about a particular topic. To draw attention to students who know a lot about a certain topic, post a reference list that states, "If you want to know more about _____, talk to _____."

> **Morning Message Sample**
>
> Nonfiction!
>
> **If you could write a nonfiction book about anything, what topic would you choose?**
>
> Fill a chart with the students' responses. Post the chart to guide students as they are selecting topics for their own nonfiction pieces.

MORNING MESSAGE IDEA: NARROWING NONFICTION TOPICS 🔦

When you ask children to make a list of nonfiction topics that they would like to research and write about, they often state broad topic areas such as snakes, fossils, polar bears, and so on. It is important that our students begin to learn how to narrow broad topics and streamline their research in order to craft a more focused piece. Guided practice in narrowing a topic is a perfect fit for the morning message. Certainly, working together to narrow a topic is much easier to do when the subject is one that your students have studied, which allows them to draw on their background knowledge.

> **Morning Message Sample**
>
> Narrowing Nonfiction Topics
>
> If you want to write about _____, how could you narrow that topic?
>
> **Broad Topic: Horses**
> 1. Kinds of horses
> 2. Caring for a horse
> 3. Riding a horse
>
> **Broad Topic: Weather**
> 1. What makes the weather?
> 2. Tools that measure/forecast weather
> 3. Thunderstorms (or other specific kinds of weather)
>
> **Broad Topic: Insects**
> 1. The parts of an insect
> 2. The life cycle of an insect
> 3. Ants (or other types of insects)

MORNING MESSAGE IDEA: CATEGORIZING NONFICTION 🌐

In addition to narrowing the topic of a nonfiction piece, it is useful if writers understand how to categorize information to form paragraphs or "chapters" of a short book. If you have a pocket chart handy, utilize it for this message. Make a list of words or phrases about an animal or other curricular-related subject. Chorally read the words or phrases, work with students to sort the facts into categories, and then agree upon a label for each category.

Morning Message Sample

Categorizing Nonfiction

Let's sort and categorize these facts about birds:
- fly
- have wings
- eat worms
- eat seeds
- nest
- chirp
- have beaks
- eat bugs
- have feathers

Let's sort and categorize these facts about bats:
- use echolocation
- sleep upside down
- live in attics
- have fur
- have claws
- fly at night
- live inside trees
- live in caves
- have ears

MORNING MESSAGE IDEA: WORD EXCHANGE ✸

See explanation on page 37.

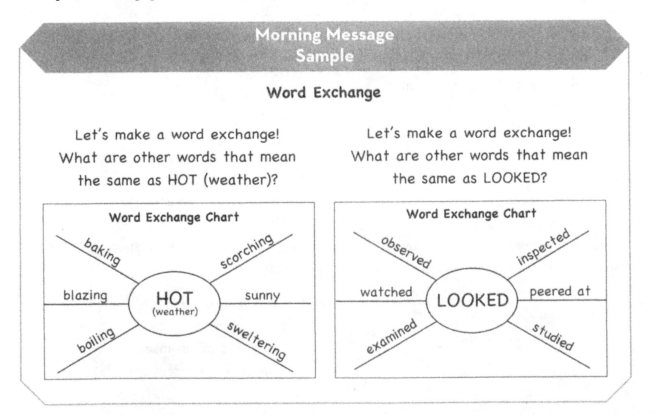

Morning Message Sample

Word Exchange

Let's make a word exchange! What are other words that mean the same as HOT (weather)?

Word Exchange Chart

baking   scorching
blazing   HOT (weather)   sunny
boiling   sweltering

Let's make a word exchange! What are other words that mean the same as LOOKED?

Word Exchange Chart

observed   inspected
watched   LOOKED   peered at
examined   studied

MORNING MESSAGE IDEA: NONFICTION ACROSTIC POEMS

If your learners are not familiar with acrostic poetry, spend a bit of time exploring mentor texts such as *Silver Seeds* (Paolilli & Brewer, 2001), which includes a collection of acrostic poems about the natural world. Use this message (in which you

explain that the subject, moon, is spelled in the poem using the first letter of each line) to summarize students' learning about a topic of their choice.

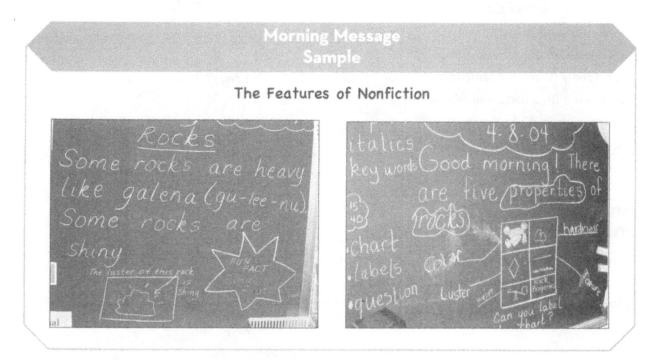

MORNING MESSAGE IDEA: THE FEATURES OF NONFICTION

To showcase the features of nonfiction texts that you and your students discover as you read and learn from these books, include selected features, such as charts, labels, pronunciation guides, and illustrations, in your message.

MORNING MESSAGE IDEA: LET'S LABEL 🌐 ?!

Post a large photo or picture from a magazine. Invite students to label all the objects that appear in the picture or the individual parts of a particular object or animal pictured.

MORNING MESSAGE IDEA: CONTRACTION MATCH 🖐

Prior to this message, familiarize your students with contractions by pointing them out during reading mini-lessons or by sending students on a contraction hunt through a piece of familiar text. Next, print the two words that make a contraction on two index cards and the contraction itself on a third card. Randomly place the words in a pocket chart. Invite students to match the two words with the proper contraction. Once all the sets are matched, work together to formulate a sentence that uses the two words, and then write the same sentence using the contraction. Orally reread the sentences. Conclude with a discussion about why an author might choose to use a contraction instead of the two words.

Morning Message Sample

Let's Label

Morning Message Sample

Contraction Match

Match the two words with the correct contraction. Use that contraction in a sentence.

do not I do not like spinach.	don't I don't like spinach.
I will I will be right there.	I'll I'll be right there.
will not He will not give me my toy back.	won't He won't give me my toy back.

MORNING MESSAGE IDEA: WRITER OF THE DAY 💬

After spending a year leading the class during the morning message, it is time to shift that responsibility to your students. To give every student a chance to write his or her own message, begin this activity when there are enough school days left so that everyone has a turn. For us, that generally means starting

Writer of the Day at the beginning of May or so. Assign each child his or her own special day and send home an explanatory letter like the one at right. If you have students whose parents are unable to help them compose a message at home, simply meet with them the morning of their assigned day to assist as they prewrite the message prior to copying it on the chalkboard or chart paper. Once the message is written, students lead the class in choral reading, editing, and rereading their message.

Morning Message Sample

Writer of the Day

Family Letter: Writer of the Day

Dear Families,

Each morning the students and I work together to write, read, revise, and edit our morning message. For the next few weeks, each child will have an opportunity to write and then lead the class in the message activities. On the back of this note you will find a calendar listing your child's day to be "Writer of the Day." On that day, your child will write his or her message on the chalkboard and lead the class in reading, editing, revising, and rereading his or her message. Please help your child prepare a message of about two to four sentences on a sheet of paper. I've included some ideas to get you started. Your child may write:

- A message with some words misspelled so the class can correct the errors
- A message leaving out consonants, vowels, blends, digraphs, or word endings
- A message with missing words (classmates will use the context of the sentence to figure out the missing words)
- A riddle
- A friendly letter
- A list of facts about his or her favorite animal
- A poem

Thank you for helping your child prepare for his or her big day!

Have fun—and happy writing!
Your Child's Teacher

MORNING MESSAGE IDEA: A FOND FAREWELL

In celebration of a year full of messages, write a final, gigantic message to wish your learners a fond farewell.

Morning Message: A Fond Farewell

Read-Alouds for Writers		
Title and Author	**Brief Summary**	**Focus**
Are You a Ladybug? (Allen, 2000)	One of a series of books that answers the title question by explaining to readers what life would be like if they were that creature	Organization
Fire! The Renewal of a Forest (Godkin, 2006)	An introduction to the role fire plays in a forest	Sentence Fluency
In the Blink of an Eye (Wiesmuller, 2002)	Written in a riddle-like format, this engaging book invites children to observe the creatures in their world.	Ideas Organization: Riddles
My Light (Bang, 2004)	The story of sunlight, energy, and electricity, written from the sun's point of view	Voice: First Person
One Tiny Turtle (Davies, 2001)	Davies's alliterative language and imagery invite readers into the world of the loggerhead turtle.	Sentence Fluency
Over in the Jungle: A Rainforest Rhyme (Berkes, 2007)	Introduce your students to the animals and plants in the rain forest with this book's variation on a familiar tune.	Sentence Fluency
The Rainforest Grew All Around (Mitchell, 2007)	Travel from the rain forest floor up to the canopy while singing to the tune of "The Green Grass Grew All Around."	Sentence Fluency
Rain, Rain, Rain Forest (Guiberson, 2004)	Take a journey through the rain forest and meet the plants and animals that live there. The book is filled with onomatopoeia!	Word Choice
A Seed Is Sleepy (Aston, 2007)	Learn about seeds and plants through Aston's poetic text and Sylvia Long's breathtaking illustrations.	Sentence Fluency
Water Dance (Locker, 1997)	This beautifully illustrated book is packed with facts about the water cycle written as riddles. It also works well for Readers Theater.	Sentence Fluency Organization: Riddles

Part 2: A Menu of Mini-Lessons—Examining the Features of Nonfiction

The mini-lessons found here zero in on the main structural difference between fiction and nonfiction—the way it is organized. Certainly, the authors of fascinating nonfiction texts employ similar techniques as those used by fiction writers, but the format in which they present the information and the features that they include to enhance the written text make nonfiction writing unique. Let's take a peek at the world of nonfiction writing.

MINI-LESSON: THE WIDE WORLD OF NONFICTION

PREPARATION: Assemble a set of five or six different types of nonfiction texts about the same topic, such as the one found in the chart below. As you read each text, note the author's unique choices, such as what facets of the topic the book describes, how the book is organized, and which nonfiction features the author uses to enhance his or her words.

A Set of Nonfiction Texts About Rocks	
Cool Rocks (Kompelien, 2007)	A how-to book on rock collecting
Dave's Down-to-Earth Rock Shop (Murphy, 2000)	A narrative nonfiction book focusing on classifying rocks in different ways
I Am a Rock (Marzollo, 1998)	A first-person account from the rock's point of view
If You Find a Rock (Christian, 2000)	A poetic text that tells about the many different types of rocks you can find
Let's Go Rock Collecting (Gans, 1997)	A descriptive book that covers the formation, characteristics, and uses of rocks

EXPLANATION: Nonfiction texts are written about a plethora of subjects and organized in many different ways. To launch a study of nonfiction, introduce students to their options as writers.

DEMONSTRATION: After reading each mentor text, discuss the way the author chose to write about the topic and how he or she organized the ideas, used specific nonfiction text features, and employed any other unique writing techniques. Record students' observations on a large index card to tuck inside or post next to the book for future reference. During your demonstration, verbalize the choices you are making as you begin a nonfiction piece.

INVITATION: "Writers, you have many choices when it comes to writing a nonfiction piece. First, you must decide what you will write about, and then think about the best way to present this information to your reader. As you begin your own nonfiction piece, think about what you've learned from the mentor texts we've read thus far."

MINI-LESSON: THE FEATURES OF NONFICTION TEXTS, PART 1 🌐

PREPARATION: Select nonfiction texts that include features such as labels, captions, boldface or colored print, headings, close-ups, maps, and so on. You will need at least one book for each student; also have sticky notes available.

EXPLANATION: This lesson is designed to set the stage for an in-depth look at nonfiction features. It puts the students in charge of noticing and beginning to name the features nonfiction writers and illustrators employ to boost readers' understanding of the content.

Types of Print	Help the reader by signaling 'Look at me'
Captions	Help the reader better understand a picture
Labels	Help the reader identify a picture
Maps	Help the reader understand where things are
Graph	Helps the reader understand mathematical information
Close-Ups	Help the reader see details in something small
Index	An A.B.C list of almost everything in the book
Glossary	

Record the features on sentence strips and place them in a pocket chart.

DEMONSTRATION: Model doing a "picture walk" through a nonfiction text. For this lesson you are not reading the words—instead, you are reading the pictures and highlighting any features you find along the way. Pause to mark a feature with a sticky note, and then discuss why the author or illustrator might have included it on the page.

INVITATION: "Researchers, now it is your turn! I'm going to give you three sticky notes. Take a picture walk through your nonfiction text and mark the features that you find. When I give the signal, we will come back to share our discoveries!" As students share their findings, list the features on a sheet of chart paper or individual sentence strips.

> ### Nonfiction Series With Prominent Features
>
> PM Animal Facts: Animals in the Wild (Rigby PM Collection)
> Science Vocabulary Readers (Scholastic)
> Windows on Literacy (science and social studies titles, National Geographic)
> World Discovery Science Readers (Scholastic)

MINI-LESSON: THE FEATURES OF NONFICTION TEXTS, PART 2—ZOOMING IN ON SPECIFIC FEATURES (CAPTIONS)

PREPARATION:

- Find a book such as *Knut: How One Little Polar Bear Captivated the World* (Hatkoff, Hatkoff, Hatkoff, & Uhlich, 2007) that showcases photographs accompanied by well-written captions.

- Locate a set of wordless picture cards. You may use picture cards designed for vocabulary lessons, photos from old calendars, or a set of "Language Cards" from your speech and language pathologist. To make your own picture cards, download clip-art photos available on the Internet.

EXPLANATION: Depending on your grade level and the amount of experience your students have had with nonfiction features, you may decide to spend a few days or a week focusing on individual features. This mini-lesson, which focuses on captions, is easily replicated for a similar in-depth study of other features. Another tactic to draw young writers' attention to the purpose of a particular feature is to select 12 to 15 texts that include the same feature. Pair students and provide each pair with a book and a large sticky note. After finding the assigned feature in the book, partners will record the answer to a sentence such as one of these:

- This map shows . . .
- This word is bold/colored because . . .
- These labels show . . .

DEMONSTRATION: Say, "Let's revisit the book *Knut* to see how the authors used captions to provide more information." Read and discuss the captions.

INVITATION: "Caption experts, I have a challenge for you. I am going to give you a picture. Look carefully at the picture, and then write a caption that explains what is happening. Once your caption is complete, you may continue your piece of writing. Can you find a place to add a picture with a caption to your own writing?"

Students create their own captions.

MINI-LESSON: THE FEATURES OF NONFICTION TEXTS, PART 3— COLLECTING OR DRAWING THEIR OWN NONFICTION FEATURES

PREPARATION:

- Copy a supply of nonfiction feature pages found in Appendix A14 on page 187.
- If you subscribe to a classroom newspaper such as *Scholastic News*, reserve a few class sets that contain the specific features you want children to collect.

EXPLANATION: After zooming in on a specific feature, students create a page for a reference booklet to use as they include that feature in their own writing. To complete the page, students record the type of feature and its purpose. Then, they draw or glue a sample of that feature on the page.

DEMONSTRATION: Model creating your own nonfiction feature page similar to the example at right.

INVITATION: "Today I would like you to draw your own illustration and create a caption to match. Also, find a sample of a caption in *Scholastic News* to glue to the back of your page. Finally, write the purpose for that feature at the bottom of the page."

Meghana draws and labels a picture of herself on her Nonfiction Feature page.

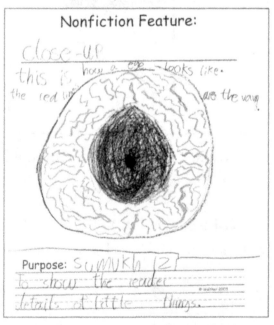

This is how a [an] eye looks like. The red lines are the veins.

MINI-LESSON: EXPOSITORY TEXT STRUCTURES

PREPARATION: Browse through your collection of nonfiction books to locate mentor texts for the text structures charted on page 156. Use a sticky note to label each book with the type of text structure so that students can refer to them as they write.

EXPLANATION: To focus this mini-lesson for young nonfiction writers, we've selected three easily replicated text structures that children can use when writing their own expository text. A more in-depth look at text structures can be found in *Literature Is Back!* (Fuhler & Walther, 2007).

DEMONSTRATION: After reading a book that exemplifies one specific text structure, discuss and chart the organizational framework.

Mentor Texts for Expository Text Structures		
Text Structure	**Title**	**Summary**
Description	*All About Sharks* (Arnosky, 2003)	One of a series of descriptive books about animals that includes, among others, alligators, deer, frogs, and lizards
	Bugs Are Insects (Rockwell, 2001)	An introduction to the fascinating world of bugs
Sequence	*Mystery Fish: Secrets of the Coelacanth* (Walker, 2006)	The fascinating story of a strange fish begins in 1938 and continues until 2002.
	What Happens to a Hamburger? (Showers, 2001)	A journey through the human digestive system
Question and Answer	*What's Up, What's Down?* (Schaefer, 2002)	Answer questions along the way as you read this unique book from bottom to top, then top to bottom.
	Thunderstorms (Doeden, 2008)	Doeden incorporates questions and answers into the text (an easy-to-read nonfiction book from a series called Pull Ahead Books: Forces of Nature, published by Lerner).

INVITATION: "Writers, today we learned about the _____ text structure. As you reread your work, think about how you have organized your text."

MINI-LESSON: NONFICTION POETRY

PREPARATION: Collect and share a sampling of poems about various topics.

Nonfiction Poetry Books	
Comets, Stars, the Moon, and Mars (Florian, 2007)	Twenty poems about the universe, including an individual poem about each planet
Mammalabilia (Florian, 2000)	A collection of unique and interesting animal poems
Scien-trickery: Riddles in Science (Lewis, 2004)	Introduce students to science topics with Lewis's lively rhyming-verse riddles.
Spectacular Science (Hopkins, 1999)	Hopkins has collected poems about topics such as snowflakes, stars, and seeds.

EXPLANATION: Poetry is yet another way for writers to present information to a reader.

DEMONSTRATION: Model writing a poem about a selected topic.

INVITATION: "Writers, remember poetry is another way you can share facts with your reader. You might want to experiment with poetry writing by taking one of the topics you've been writing about and turning it into a poem."

MINI-LESSON: LET'S PRETEND

PREPARATION: Scholastic publishes a collection of Hello Reader! Science books written by Jean Marzollo and illustrated by Judith Moffatt that are a perfect fit for this lesson. The series includes the following titles.

I Am a Leaf (1998)	*I Am Planet Earth* (2000)	*I Am a Star* (2000)
I Am Snow (1998)	*I Am an Apple* (1997)	*I Am Water* (1996)
I Am Fire (1996)	*I'm a Caterpillar* (1997)	

EXPLANATION: When you watch your students as they play during recess, what do they do? We often observe our first graders pretending to be someone or something else. One day it might be their favorite pet, the next day a video game hero. Children use their imaginative lives to gain a deeper understanding of the world. As primary teachers, we can capitalize on children's vivid imaginations and desire to pretend while at the same time introducing them to the world of nonfiction writing.

DEMONSTRATION: Research and build background about a particular curricular-related topic by reading nonfiction books aloud and recording facts on a chart. Engage in the following discussion with your students: "Today when I watched you on the playground I noticed that many of you were pretending to be something else. Can anyone tell me about who or what you were pretending to be?" Pause to get responses. "Wow! Isn't our imagination an amazing thing! Today we are going to use our imagination and pretend we are _____. Then we are going to use the facts that we've learned from our research to write a teaching book about _____." Collect students' ideas in the pocket chart or on chart paper.

INVITATION: "Authors, let's write about _____ from the first-person point of view just like Jean Marzollo did in her books!"

Collect students' ideas in a pocket chart.

MINI-LESSON: GRABBING YOUR READER'S ATTENTION 🌑 ✳

PREPARATION:

- Collect and share a number of nonfiction books with great "grabbers."
- Create a chart of "grabbers" to post in your classroom.

EXPLANATION: Engaging nonfiction texts begin with a well-crafted opening that grabs readers and compels them to continue. The mini-lesson is similar to What Kind of Lead Do I Need? on page 80.

A Collection of Great
GRABBERS!
See the _____ up in the sky. Watch
it as it _____ by!
_____ fill our world with beauty
and grace.
Yikes! _____ look scary close up. But
you don't need to worry.
_____ here, _____ there, _____
creeping everywhere!
There are many kinds of _____ living
all around us.

A list of great grabbers

Nonfiction Books With Great "Grabbers"	
Almost Gone: The World's Rarest Animals (Jenkins, 2006)	A concise paragraph about an endangered animal appears on each page. Every paragraph grabs the reader's attention in a unique way.
The Search for Antarctic Dinosaurs (Walker, 2008)	"Rocks, ice, and snow. At first, that was all Dr. William Hammer and his crew saw when they looked at the land around them."
Our Wet World (Collard, 1998)	"Don't look now, but we're surrounded. Yes, you and I are surrounded by the most abundant liquid on earth—water."

DEMONSTRATION: Say, "Now that we've written down a few different ways that authors begin a nonfiction book, do you notice any familiar techniques?" Some students may notice that Sally Walker launched her book with a list. For your demonstration, choose a topic, and then pen a few grabbers.

INVITATION: "Authors, think about the approaches the authors took to grabbing their readers. Experiment with different techniques in your writing. You may want to take a few moments at the beginning of the workshop to write a grabber sentence or two."

MINI-LESSON: TOPIC SENTENCES 🌐 🌐

PREPARATION: Find books in which the author has effectively used topic sentences.

- *Animal Dads* (Collard, 1997). Collard launches each page with a clear topic sentence to describe how males of different species take care of their young.

- *Flashy Fantastic Rain Forest Frogs* (Patent, 1997). Each page of this well-written book has a topic sentence and supporting details.

EXPLANATION: A topic sentence sets the purpose for the piece by introducing or previewing the topic for the reader. This mini-lesson serves as an introduction and should be followed by continued study of topic sentences in mentor texts and multiple demonstrations.

DEMONSTRATION: Say, "Writers, when you are trying to write a topic sentence, ask yourself, 'What is this part going to be about?' Once you've figured that out, you need to write a sentence announcing the topic to your readers. Let me show you what I mean. If I were going to write a piece about _____, my topic sentence might be _____." Continue by crafting effective topic sentences.

INVITATION: "Authors, as you reread your work today, see if you've set the stage for your reader by including a topic sentence. If not, consider going back to revise your piece to include one."

MINI-LESSON: SYNONYM BINGO

PREPARATION:

- If students are not familiar with the term *synonym*, introduce it by reading *If You Were a Synonym* (Dahl, 2007).
- Create a list of words for students to write. Make and copy a nine-square synonym bingo card for each child. Choose words from the Word Exchange lessons found in each chapter.
- Write the list on the board and instruct students to write each word in a square on their card in random order.
- Pass out cubes or chips for students to mark their cards.
- Write the synonyms on index cards and place in a container. Draw one word at a time. Students mark the word on their bingo card that is the synonym of the word you called. Continue in the same manner until a child has bingo.

EXPLANATION: We like to have a few writing-related games to play on the last days of school, so we've included game ideas in the last three mini-lessons. Enjoy! This particular game reviews all the words that you've explored during your Word Exchange lessons.

DEMONSTRATION: Explain the rules of the game.

INVITATION: "Let's play Synonym Bingo!"

MINI-LESSON: GRAMMAR REVIEW GAMES

PREPARATION: Prepare materials for the game of your choice.

- **Grammar Race:** Prepare individual index cards or "flash cards" with words that are nouns, verbs, or adjectives. Provide each student with a place to quickly record his or her response—individual slates or whiteboards work well. To play the game, set a timer for five minutes.

Flash a word card, and have students indicate the part of speech on their slate by writing the letter N, V, or A. Continue until the timer sounds. Count how many parts of speech your students identified in five minutes.

- **Parts of Speech Pictionary**: Prepare individual index cards with words that are nouns, verbs, or adjectives. Divide the class into two teams. A player on one team selects a card, states the part of speech, and then draws a picture of that item for his or her teammates to identify. Then, the next team takes a turn.
- **Charades**: Prepare individual index cards with words that are nouns, verbs, or adjectives. A student chooses a card, identifies the part of speech, and then acts it out for the class to guess.

DEMONSTRATION: Explain the rules of the game.

INVITATION: "Let's play a grammar game!"

MINI-LESSON: CONVENTIONS REVIEW—A PUNCTUATION BEE ?!

PREPARATION:

- Read and discuss *Penny and the Punctuation Bee* (Donohue, 2008), in which Penny the period is determined to win this year's punctuation bee. Will she triumph over the reigning champion, Elsie the exclamation mark?

- Divide the class into three teams, one for each punctuation mark (period, question mark, and exclamation mark) or if those teams are too large, six smaller teams, two for each mark.
- Write an assortment of nouns on large index cards.

EXPLANATION: To play the game, show a word card to the class. Each team works together to compose and then write a sentence using its mark. If the sentence is correctly punctuated, the team wins a point. Continue with more words in the same fashion.

DEMONSTRATION: Explain the rules of the game.

INVITATION: "Punctuation experts, let's have our own punctuation bee!"

Part 3: Genre Exploration: Delving Into Nonfiction— From Research to Writing 🅐

EXPLANATION

For the final genre exploration of the year, students put everything they have learned during the mini-lessons to use as they create a nonfiction piece. For the day-by-day plan (see page 162), the students researched and wrote about animals. The broad topic you choose will be based on your curriculum and available resources. To provide additional structure and support to this series of mini-lessons, poll students about their preferred topic. Organize students into pairs or triads according to their preferences and ability. For instance, if four students want to research and write about sharks, make two partnerships by pairing the two students with more advanced writing skills with the two students who may need a bit of support. Collect and store their books and materials in a plastic bag for easy access during writing workshop.

April & May Genre Exploration Chart Delving Into Nonfiction: From Research to Writing		
Kid-Friendly Definition of Genre: A nonfiction piece tells the reader facts about people, animals, places, or events.		
Characteristics of Genre: • Gives information • Written to inform, explain, or persuade • Factually accurate • Sometimes written in narrative format • May use features to communicate information		
Mentor Texts		
K	**1**	**2**
Nonfiction texts to read aloud	An assortment of nonfiction texts about animals	Scholastic Science Vocabulary Readers
Zooming In to Align Instruction Across the Grades		
K—Shared or Interactive Writing	**1—All About Animals**	**2—Fact Finders**
Follow the day-by-day plan found on page 162 in a shared or interactive writing format, working together to research and write a nonfiction text. Once written, make a copy for each student to illustrate and add appropriate nonfiction features.	See day-by-day plan on page 162.	• Choose a topic. • Research the topic to collect facts. • Categorize the facts into four or more sections. • Organize the facts in each section. • Write a multi-paragraph page about each category, including pertinent features of nonfiction. • Revise, edit, polish, and present.

A DAY-BY-DAY PLAN FOR A NONFICTION PIECE ABOUT ANIMALS

PREPARATION: To guide your students as they write a nonfiction piece about animals you will need the following:

- Nonfiction books, magazines, or other information sources about a topic of interest to your students. *ZOO-BOOKS* magazines work well for studying animals.
- Unlined paper divided into fourths for collecting "dash facts"
- Nonfiction booklet (see Appendix A15, pages 188–190)

A research team works together to learn about sharks.

Mini-Lesson 1:

Begin by choosing a topic you want to research and write about by thinking aloud in front of students. Create four categories, such as Looks Like, Home, Favorite Foods, and Fun Facts to organize your information. After your demonstration, pass out student materials and provide time for them to explore and discuss the nonfiction books.

Mini-Lessons 2–4:

Demonstrate how to collect "dash facts" on a piece of chart paper folded into fourths. The idea of dash facts comes from a lesson found in the book *Nonfiction Craft Lessons: Teaching Information Writing K–8* (Portalupi & Fletcher, 2001). Dash facts are simply quick facts written in short phrases.

Owls	
Looks Like	**Home**
• feathers	• cold places
• pointy beak	• jungles
• 4 talons, 2 legs	• forest
• long wings	• near farms
• round eyes	• in trees
Favorite Foods	**Fun Facts**
• mice	• heads turn almost all the way around
• other small rodents	• spit out owl pellets
	• fly silently

You may want to model one or two categories each day.

Mini-Lessons 5–7:

Model how to turn dash facts into complete sentences. Demonstrate this with one or two categories each day, purposefully modeling the

Young researchers record their "dash facts."

techniques you've studied in mentor texts. Each day, students use dash facts to write complete sentences in their nonfiction book.

Mini-Lessons 8–10:

Revise, edit, polish, and celebrate!

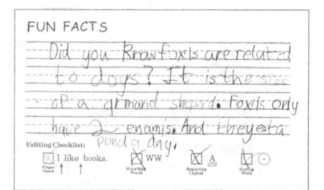

A fox has reeeeally sharp teeth. And a really long snout. And a biiiig bushy tail. And great big ears for hearing.

Foxes usually (you-zolee) live in forests, meadows, dens, and grasslands. These places have the best food! Turn the page to learn about what they eat!

A fox eats fruit, opposums, hares, and small animals. The places where foxes live have the perfect amount of food for the foxes.

Did you know foxes are related to dogs? It is the size of a German Shepard. Foxes only have 2 enemies. And they eat a pound a day.

Final Thoughts

We did it! We nurtured our learners through beginning-of-the-year tears and enthusiastically joined them in end-of-the-year cheers! The completion of a school year offers one last opportunity for looking back and looking forward. Ask yourself, "As I plan for next year, how can I continue to improve my writing instruction?" What will you do again and what will you change? Know that we will be joining you in that endeavor as we continue to reflect on our students' learning, refine our lessons, and improve our instruction. Celebrate, relax, and recharge. School will begin again before we know it.

References

Professional References Cited

Bellamy, P. C. (Ed.). (2005). *Seeing with new eyes: Using the 6 + 1 trait model* (6th ed.). Portland, OR: NWREL.

Button, K., Johnson, M. J., & Furgerson, P. (1996). Interactive writing in the primary classroom. *The Reading Teacher, 49*(6), 446–454.

Clarke, L. K. (1988). Invented versus traditional spelling in first graders' writings: Effects on learning to spell and read. *Research in the Teaching of English, 22*, 281–309.

Culham, R. (2005). *6+1 traits of writing: The complete guide for the primary grades.* New York: Scholastic.

_____. (2006). The trait lady speaks up. *Educational Leadership, 64*(2), 53–57.

_____. (2008). *Inside the writing traits classroom: K–2 lessons on DVD.* New York: Scholastic.

Culham, R., & Coutu, R. (2008). *Using picture books to teach writing with the traits.* New York: Scholastic.

Cunningham, P. M. (2009). *Phonics they use: Words for reading and writing* (5th ed.). Boston: Pearson/Allyn & Bacon.

Cunningham, P. M., & Hall, D. (2002). *Month-by-month phonics for first grade: Systematic, multilevel instruction for first grade.* Greensboro, NC: Four Blocks/Carson-Dellosa.

Farris, P. J. (2005). *Language arts: Process, product, and assessment* (4th ed.). Long Grove, IL: Waveland.

Essley, R. (2008). *Visual tools for differentiating reading and writing instruction.* New York: Scholastic.

Fletcher, R., & Portalupi, J. (2001). *Writing workshop: The essential guide.* Portsmouth, NH: Heinemann.

Fountas, I. C., & Pinnell, G. S. (1996). *Guided reading: Good first teaching for all children.* Portsmouth, NH: Heinemann.

Fry, E. B. (1998). Teaching reading: The most common phonograms. *The Reading Teacher, 51*(7), 620–622.

Fuhler, C. J., & Walther, M. P. (2007). *Literature is back! Using the best books for teaching readers and writers across genres.* New York: Scholastic.

Galda, L., & Cullinan, B. E. (2003). Literature for literacy. What research says about the benefits of using trade books in the classroom. In J. Flood, D. Lapp, J. R. Squire, & J. M. Jensen (Eds.), *Handbook of research on teaching the English language arts* (2nd ed.) (pp. 640–648). Old Tappan, NJ: Macmillan.

Graves, D. (1983). *Writing: Teachers and children at work.* Exeter, NH: Heinemann.

Hall, D., & Cunningham, P. M. (2001). *Month-by-month phonics for second grade: Systematic, multilevel instruction for second grade.* Greensboro, NC: Four Blocks/Carson-Dellosa.

Harvey, S., & Goudvis, A. (2000). *Strategies that work: Teaching comprehension to enhance understanding.* Portland, ME: Stenhouse.

Hoyt, L. (1999). *Revisit, reflect, retell: Strategies for improving reading comprehension.* Portsmouth, NH: Heinemann.

_____. (2000). *Snapshots: Literacy minilessons up close.* Portsmouth, NH: Heinemann.

Johnston, P. H. (2004). *Choice words.* Portland, ME: Stenhouse.

McCarrier, A., Pinnell, G. S., & Fountas, I. C. (2000). *Interactive writing: How language and literacy come together, K–2.* Portsmouth, NH: Heinemann.

McMahon, C., & Warrick, P. (2005). *Wee can write: Using 6 + 1 trait writing strategies with renowned children's literature.* Portland, OR: NWREL.

Miller, D. (2002). *Reading with meaning: Teaching comprehension in the primary grades.* Portland, ME: Stenhouse.

Northwest Regional Educational Laboratory. (1999). *Seeing with new eyes: A guidebook on teaching and assessing beginning writers* (5th ed.). Portland, OR: Author.

Portalupi, J., & Fletcher, R. (2001). *Nonfiction craft lessons: Teaching information writing K–8.* Portland, ME: Stenhouse.

Ray, K. W., with Cleaveland, L. B. (2004). *About the authors: Writing workshop with our youngest writers.* Portsmouth, NH: Heinemann.

Ray, K. W., with Laminack, L. (2001). *The writing workshop: Working through the hard parts (and they're all hard parts).* Urbana, IL: NCTE.

Rickards, D., & Hawes, S. (2006). Connecting reading and writing through author's craft. *The Reading Teacher, 60*(4), 370–373.

Robb, L. (2004). *Nonfiction writing: From the inside out.* New York: Scholastic.

Routman, R. (2005). *Writing essentials.* Portsmouth, NH: Heinemann.

Saddler, B. (2005). Sentence combining: A sentence-level writing intervention. *The Reading Teacher, 58*(5), 468–471.

Smith, M. W., & Wilhelm, J. (2006). What research tells us about teaching grammar. *Voices from the Middle, 13*(4), 40–43.

Spandel, V. (2004). *Creating young writers: Using the six traits to enrich writing process in primary classrooms.* Boston: Allyn & Bacon.

_____. (2008). *Creating young writers: Using the six traits to enrich writing process in primary grades* (2nd ed.). Boston: Allyn & Bacon.

Stead, T. (2002). *Is that a fact? Teaching nonfiction writing K–3.* Portland, ME: Stenhouse.

Children's Literature Cited

Chapter 2: September

Banks, K. (2008). *Max's dragon.* (B. Kulikov, Illus.). New York: Farrar, Straus and Giroux.

Barracca, D., & Barracca, S. (1990). *The adventures of Taxi Dog.* (M. Buehner, Illus.). New York: Dial.

_____. (1991). *Maxi, the hero.* (M. Buehner, Illus.). New York: Dial.

_____. (1993). *Maxi, the star.* (A. Ayers, Illus.). New York: Dial.

Barrett, J. (1998). *Things that are most in the world.* (J. Nickle, Illus.). New York: Atheneum.

Beaumont, K. (2004). *I like myself!* (D. Catrow, Illus.). Orlando, FL: Harcourt.

Brown, M. (2007). *My name is Gabito: The life of Gabriel García Márquez.* (R. Colón, Illus.). Flagstaff, AZ: Rising Moon.

Brown, M. (1996). *Arthur writes a story.* New York: Little, Brown.

Bunting, E. (2003). *Anna's table.* Chanhassen, MN: Northword.

Bush, L., & Bush, J. (2008). *Read all about it!* (D. Brunkus, Illus.). New York: HarperCollins.

Carlson, N. L. (1988). *I like me!* New York: Viking.

_____. (2004). *There's a big, beautiful world out there!* New York: Puffin.

Cleary, B. P. (1999). *A mink, a fink, a skating rink: What is a noun?* (J. Prosmitsky, Illus.). Minneapolis, MN: Carolrhoda.

Cocca-Leffler, M. (1999). *Mr. Tanen's ties.* Morton Grove, IL: A. Whitman.

Dahl, M. (2006). *If you were a noun.* (S. Gray, Illus.). Minneapolis, MN: Picture Window.

Frame, J. A. (2003). *Yesterday I had the blues.* (R. G. Christie, Illus.). Berkeley, CA: Tricycle.

Ginsburg, M. (1972). *The chick and the duckling.* (J. & A. Aruego, Illus.). New York: Macmillan.

Kachenmeister, C. (2001). *On Monday when it rained.* (T. Berthiaume, Illus.). Boston: Houghton Mifflin.

Lester, H. (1997). *Author: A true story.* Boston: Houghton Mifflin.

Martin, B., Jr. (1967). *Brown bear, brown bear, what do you see?* (E. Carle, Illus.). New York: Holt.

O'Connor, J. (2008). *Fancy Nancy: Bonjour, butterfly.* (R. P. Glasser, Illus.). New York: HarperCollins.

Perkins, L. R. (2007). *Pictures from our vacation.* New York: Greenwillow.

Pinkwater, D. M. (1977). *The big orange splot.* New York: Hastings House.

Pulver, R. (2003). *Punctuation takes a vacation.* (L. R. Reed, Illus.). New York: Holiday House.

Reynolds, P. H. (2004). *Ish.* New York: Candlewick.

Roberts, S. (2003). *We all go traveling by.* (S. Bell, Illus.). Cambridge, MA: Barefoot Books.

Root, P. (2003). *The name quilt.* (M. Apple, Illus.). New York: Farrar, Straus and Giroux.

Rylant, C. (2004). *Mr. Putter and Tabby write the book.* (A. Howard, Illus.). New York: Harcourt.

Seuss, Dr. (1996). *My many colored days.* (S. Johnson & L. Fancher, Illus.). New York: Knopf.

Sierra, J. (2004). *Wild about books.* (M. Brown, Illus.). New York: Knopf.

Viorst, J. (1972). *Alexander and the terrible, horrible, no good, very bad day.* (R. Cruz, Illus.). New York: Atheneum.

Wong, J. S. (2002). *You have to write.* New York: Margaret K. McElderry.

Wood, D. (2002). *A quiet place.* New York: Simon & Schuster.

Zemach, K. (2008). *Ms. McCaw learns to draw.* New York: Arthur A. Levine/Scholastic.

Ziefert, H. (2001). *39 uses for a friend.* (R. Doughty, Illus.). New York: Putnam.

Chapter 3: October

Andrews, S. (1995). *Rattlebone rock.* (J. Plecas, Illus.). New York: HarperCollins.

Aruego, J. (2006). *The last laugh*. (A. Dewey, Illus.). New York: Dial.

Banks, K. (2006). *Max's words*. (B. Kulikov, Illus.). New York: Farrar, Straus and Giroux.

Calmenson, S. (1993). *It begins with an A*. (M. Russo, Illus.). New York: Hyperion.

Cleary, B. P. (2001). *To root, to toot, to parachute: What is a verb?* (J. Prosmitsky, Illus.). Minneapolis, MN: Carolrhoda.

Cazet, D. (1990). *Never spit on your shoes*. New York: Orchard.

DiCamillo, K. (2007). *Mercy Watson: Princess in disguise*. (C. Van Dusen, Illus.). Cambridge, MA: Candlewick.

Dahl, M. (2006). *If you were a verb*. (S. Gray, Illus.). Minneapolis, MN: Picture Window.

Davis, K. (1998). *Who hops?* San Diego: Harcourt.

_____. (2000). *Who hoots?* San Diego: Harcourt.

Donaldson, J. (2001). *Room on the broom*. (A. Scheffler, Illus.). New York: Dial.

Finchler, J. (1995). *Miss Malarkey doesn't live in room 10*. (K. O'Malley, Illus.). New York: Walker.

Franson, S. E. (2007). *Un-brella*. New Millford, CT: Roaring Brook.

Frazee, M., et al. (2006). *Why did the chicken cross the road?* New York: Dial.

Freyman, S., et al. (2007). *Knock, knock!* New York: Dial.

Friend, C. (2007). *The perfect nest*. (J. Manders, Illus.). Cambridge, MA: Candlewick.

Grogan, J. (2007). *Bad dog, Marley!* (R. Cowdrey, Illus.). New York: HarperCollins.

Helakoski, L. (2008). *Woolbur*. (L. Harper, Illus.). New York: HarperCollins.

Jenkins, S., & Page, R. (2006). *Move!* Boston: Houghton Mifflin.

_____. (2003). *What do you do with a tail like this?* Boston: Houghton Mifflin.

Kasza, K. (1987). *The wolf's chicken stew*. New York: Putnam.

Kraus, R. (1986). *Where are you going, little mouse?* (J. Aruego & A. Dewey, Illus.). New York: Greenwillow.

Lee, S. (2008). *Wave*. New York: Chronicle.

Lehman, B. (2006). *Museum trip*. Boston: Houghton Mifflin.

_____. (2007). *Rainstorm*. Boston: Houghton Mifflin.

Luthardt, K. (2003). *Peep!* Atlanta: Peachtree.

Munsch, R. (1980). *The paper bag princess*. (M. Martchenko, Illus.). Toronto, Ontario: Annick.

Newgarden, M., & Cash, M. M. (2007). *Bow-Wow bugs a bug*. Orlando, FL: Harcourt.

Nikola-Lisa, W. (1997). *Shake dem Halloween bones*. (M. Reed, Illus.). Boston: Houghton Mifflin.

O'Malley, K. (2005). *Once upon a cool motorcycle dude*. (K. O'Malley, C. Heyer, & S. Goto, Illus.). New York: Walker.

Pulver, R. (2006). *Nouns and verbs have a field day*. (L. R. Reed, Illus.). New York: Holiday House.

Schneider, R. M. (1995). *Add it, dip it, fix it: A book of verbs*. Boston: Houghton Mifflin.

Taylor, S. (2006). *When a monster is born*. (N. Sharratt, Illus.). New Millford, CT: Roaring Brook.

Turkle, B. (1976). *Deep in the forest*. New York: Dutton.

Van Dusen, C. (2005). *If I built a car*. New York: Dutton.

Walker, S. M. (2008). *The vowel family: A tale of lost letters*. (K. Luthardt, Illus.). Minneapolis. MN: Carolrhoda.

Williams, L. (1986). *The little old lady who was not afraid of anything*. (M. Lloyd, Illus.). New York: Crowell.

Chapter 4: November and December

Bateman, T. (2004). *A plump and perky turkey*. (J. Shelly, Illus.). New York: Marshall Cavendish.

Bloom, B. (1999). *Wolf!* (P. Biet, Illus.). New York: Orchard.

Boynton, S. (1987). *A is for angry: An animal and adjective alphabet*. New York: Workman.

Brett, J. (1999). *Gingerbread baby*. New York: Putnam.

Brown, M. (1989). *Arthur's birthday*. Boston: Little, Brown.

Bullard, L. (2007). *You can write a story! A story-writing recipe for kids*. (D. H. Melmon, Illus.). Minnetonka, MN: Two-Can.

Bunting, E. (2007). *Hurry! Hurry!* (J. Mack, Illus.). New York: Harcourt.

Cannon, J. (1993). *Stellaluna*. San Diego: Harcourt.

Cleary, B. P. (2000). *Hairy, scary, ordinary: What is an adjective?* (J. Prosmitsky, Illus.). Minneapolis, MN: Carolrhoda.

Clement, R. (1997). *Grandpa's teeth*. New York: HarperCollins.

Coleman, M. (2000). *A silly snowy day*. (G. Williamson, Illus.). New York: Scholastic.

Cronin, D. (2000). *Click, clack, moo: Cows that type*. (B. Lewis, Illus.). New York: Simon & Schuster.

Dahl, M. (2006). *If you were an adjective*. (S. Gray, Illus.). Minneapolis, MN: Picture Window.

Donaldson, J. (1999). *The gruffalo*. (A. Scheffler, Illus.). New York: Dial.

Duke, K. (1992). *Aunt Isabel tells a good one*. New York: Dutton.

Eaton, M. (2007). *Best buds*. New York: Knopf.

_____. (2007). *Superheroes*. New York: Knopf.

Ehrlich, A. (1989). *Rapunzel*. (K. Waldherr, Illus.). New York: Dial.

Fleming, C. (2002). *Muncha! Muncha! Muncha!* (G. B. Karas, Illus.). New York: Atheneum.

_____. (2003). *Boxes for Katje*. (S. Dressen-McQueen, Illus.). New York: Farrar, Straus and Giroux.

Galdone, P. (1973). *The little red hen*. New York: Clarion.

_____. (1975). *The gingerbread boy*. New York: Clarion.

Gerstein, M. (2007). *Leaving the nest*. New York: Farrar, Straus and Giroux.

Goldfinger, J. P. (2007). *My dog Lyle*. New York: Clarion.

Hatkoff, I., Hatkoff, C., & Kahumbu, P. (2006). *Owen & Mzee: The true story of a remarkable friendship*. (P. Greste, Photographer). New York: Scholastic.

Jackson, A. (1997). *I know an old lady who swallowed a pie*. (J. B. Schachner, Illus.). New York: Dutton.

Ji, Z. (2008). *No! That's wrong!* (C. Xu, Illus.). La Jolla, CA: Kane Miller.

Jones, C. C. (2008). *Winter white*. (T. Ouren, Illus.). Minneapolis, MN: Picture Window.

Kasza, K. (2003). *My lucky day*. New York: Putnam.

_____. (2007). *Badger's fancy meal*. New York: Putnam.

Ketteman, H. (2004). *Armadilly chili*. (W. Terry, Illus.). Morton Grove, IL: A. Whitman.

Laden, N. (1994). *The night I followed the dog*. New York: Chronicle.

Lester, H. (1988). *Tacky the penguin*. (L. Munsinger, Illus.). Boston: Houghton Mifflin.

Long, M. (2003). *How I became a pirate*. (D. Shannon, Illus.). Orlando, FL: Harcourt.

McLeod, B. (2006). *Superhero ABC*. New York: HarperCollins.

McMullan, K. (2002). *I stink!* (J. McMullan, Illus.). New York: Joanna Cotler.

_____. (2003). *I'm mighty!* (J. McMullan, Illus.). New York: Joanna Cotler.

_____. (2006). *I'm dirty!* (J. McMullan, Illus.). New York: Joanna Cotler.

Palatini, M. (2004). *Moo who?* (K. Graves, Illus.). New York: Katherine Tegen.

Paul, A. W. (2004). *Mañana, iguana*. (E. Long, Illus.). New York: Holiday House.

Perkins, L. R. (2003). *Snow music*. New York: Greenwillow.

Piven, H. (2007). *My dog is as smelly as dirty socks*. New York: Schwartz & Wade.

Rotner, S. (2008). *Senses in the city*. Minneapolis, MN: Millbrook.

Ryan, P. M. (2001). *Hello ocean*. (M. Astrella, Illus.). Watertown, MA: Charlesbridge.

Rylant, C. (2000). *In November*. (J. Kastner, Illus.). San Diego: Harcourt.

Schories, P. (2004). *Breakfast for Jack*. Ashville, NC: Front Street.

_____. (2004). *Jack and the missing piece*. Ashville, NC: Front Street.

_____. (2006). *Jack and the night visitors*. Ashville, NC: Front Street.

Squires, J. (2006). *The gingerbread cowboy*. (H. Berry, Illus.). New York: Laura Geringer.

Stevens, J., & Stevens Crummel, S. (2005). *The great fuzz frenzy*. (J. Stevens, Illus.). Orlando, FL: Harcourt.

Stringer, L. (2006). *Winter is the warmest season*. Orlando, FL: Harcourt.

Walton, R. (2001). *That's my dog!* New York: Putnam.

Wilcox, L. (2003). *Falling for Rapunzel*. (L. Monks, Illus.). New York: Putnam.

Willey, M. (2001). *Clever Beatrice: An Upper Peninsula conte*. (H. McWhorter, Illus.). New York: Atheneum.

Wood, A. (1985). *King Bidgood's in the bathtub*. (D. Wood, Illus.). San Diego: Harcourt.

Chapter 5: January

Ada, A. F. (1994). *Dear Peter Rabbit*. (L. Tryon, Illus.). New York: Atheneum.

_____. (1998). *Yours truly, Goldilocks*. (L. Tryon, Illus.). New York: Atheneum.

_____. (2001). *With love, Little Red Hen*. (L. Tryon, Illus.). New York: Atheneum.

Bottner, B., & Kruglik, G. (2004). *Wallace's lists*. (O. Landstrom, Illus.). New York: HarperCollins.

Brett, J. (1989). *The mitten: A Ukrainian folktale*. New York: Putnam.

Bruel, N. (2005). *Bad kitty*. New Millford, CT: Roaring Brook.

_____. (2007). *Poor puppy*. New Millford, CT: Roaring Brook.

Buehner, C. (2002). *Snowmen at night*. (M. Buehner, Illus.). New York: Phyllis Fogelman.

Crews, N. (2004). *The neighborhood Mother Goose*. New York: Greenwillow.

Cronin, D. (2000). *Click, clack, moo: Cows that type*. (B. Lewin, Illus.). New York: Simon & Schuster.

_____. (2002). *Giggle, giggle, quack*. (B. Lewin, Illus.). New York: Simon & Schuster.

_____. (2003). *Diary of a worm.* (H. Bliss, Illus.). New York: Joanna Cotler.

_____. (2005). *Diary of a spider.* (H. Bliss, Illus.). New York: Joanna Cotler.

Edwards, P. D. (2005). *The neat line: Scribbling through Mother Goose.* (D. C. Bluthenthal, Illus.). New York: Katherine Tegen.

Ernst, L. C. (1995). *Little Red Riding Hood: A newfangled prairie tale.* New York: Simon & Schuster.

Fanelli, S. (1995). *My map book.* New York: HarperCollins.

Fisher, C. (2008). *The snow show.* Orlando, FL: Harcourt.

Fleming, D. (2005). *The first day of winter.* New York: Holt.

Gerasole, I., & Gerasole, O. (2007). *The spatulatta cookbook.* New York: Scholastic.

Grambling, L. (1995). *Can I have a stegosaurus, Mom? Can I? Please!?* (H. B. Lewis, Illus.). Mahwah, NJ: Bridgewater.

Hershenhorn, E. (2002). *Chicken soup by heart.* (R. Litzinger, Illus.). New York: Simon & Schuster.

_____. (2009). *S is for story: A writer's alphabet.* (Z. Pullen, Illus.). Chelsea, MI: Sleeping Bear.

Hoose, P., & Hoose, H. (1998). *Hey, little ant.* (D. Tilley, Illus.). Berkeley, CA: Tricycle.

Horowitz, D. (2008). *Twenty-six princesses.* New York: Putnam.

Hutchins, P. (1968). *Rosie's walk.* New York: Simon & Schuster.

Jackson, A. (2008). *Thea's tree.* (J. Pederson, Illus.) New York: Dutton.

Johnson, D. A. (2006). *Snow sounds: An onomatopoetic story.* Boston: Houghton Mifflin.

Kloske, G. (2005). *Once upon a time, the end (asleep in 60 seconds).* (B. Blitt, Illus.). New York: Atheneum.

Leedy, L. (1993). *Postcards from Pluto: A tour of the solar system.* New York: Holiday House.

Lester, H. (1988). *Tacky the penguin.* (L. Munsinger, Illus.). Boston: Houghton Mifflin.

Lobel, A. (1972). *Frog and toad together.* New York: HarperCollins.

O'Connor, J. (2008). *Fancy Nancy's favorite fancy words: From accessories to zany.* (R. Preiss-Glasser, Illus.). New York: HarperCollins.

Peck, J. (1997). *The giant carrot.* (B. Root, Illus.). New York: Dial.

Polacco, P. (1990). *Thunder cake.* New York: Philomel.

Rappaport, D. (2001). *Martin's big words: The life of Martin Luther King, Jr.* (B. Collier, Illus.). New York: Hyperion.

Reynolds, A. (2005). *Chicks and salsa.* (P. Bogan, Illus.). New York: Bloomsbury.

Teague, M. (2002). *Dear Mrs. LaRue: Letters from obedience school.* New York: Scholastic.

Sams, C. R., & Stoick, J. (2000). *Stranger in the woods: A photographic fantasy.* Milford, MI: Carl R. Sams II Photography.

Schertle, A. (2002). *All you need for a snowman.* (B. Lavallee, Illus.). San Diego: Harcourt.

Sobel, J. (2006). *Shiver me letters: A pirate ABC.* (H. Cole, Illus.). Orlando, FL: Harcourt.

Stevens, J., & Stevens Crummel, S. (2008). *Help me, Mr. Mutt!: Expert answers for dogs with people problems.* (J. Stevens, Illus.). Orlando, FL: Harcourt.

Stewart, S. (1997). *The gardener.* (D. Small, Illus.). New York: Farrar, Straus and Giroux.

Walton, R. (2006). *Around the house the fox chased the mouse: A prepositional tale.* (J. Bradshaw, Illus.). Salt Lake City, UT: Gibbs Smith.

Weatherford, C. B. (2005). *Freedom on the menu: The Greensboro sit-ins.* (J. Lagarrigue, Illus.). New York: Penguin.

Chapter 6: February

Anderson, L. H. (2002). *Thank you, Sarah: The woman who saved Thanksgiving.* (M. Faulkner, Illus.). New York: Simon & Schuster.

Borden, L. (2000). *A. Lincoln and me.* (T. Lewin, Illus.). New York: Scholastic.

Cleary, B. P. (2006). *A lime, a mime, a pool of slime: More about nouns.* (B. Gable, Illus.). Minneapolis, MN: Millbrook.

Coles, R. (1995). *The story of Ruby Bridges.* (G. Ford, Illus.). New York: Scholastic.

deGroat, D. (1996). *Roses are pink, your feet really stink.* New York: Morrow.

Jurmain, S. T. (2006). *George did it.* (L. Day, Illus.). New York: Dutton.

Kerley, B. (2008). *What to do about Alice?* (E. Fotheringham, Illus.). New York: Scholastic.

King, C. K. (2003). *My brother Martin: A sister remembers growing up with the Rev. Dr. Martin Luther King.* (C. Soentpiet, Illus.). New York: Simon & Schuster.

Kroll, S. (2001). *Patches lost and found.* (B. Gott, Illus.). Delray Beach, FL: Winslow Press.

Murphy, F. (2002). *George Washington and the general's dog.* (R. Walz, Illus.). New York: Random House.

Pinkney, A. D. (1998). *Duke Ellington.* (B. Pinkney, Illus.). New York: Hyperion.

Rankin, L. (2006). *Fluffy and Baron*. New York: Dial.

Schanzer, R. (2003). *How Ben Franklin stole the lightning*. New York: HarperCollins.

Weatherford, C. B. (2008). *Before John was a jazz giant*. (S. Qualls, Illus.). New York: Holt.

Winnick, K. B. (1996). *Mr. Lincoln's whiskers*. Honesdale, PA: Boyds Mills.

Winter, J. (2005). *The librarian of Basra: A true story from Iraq*. Orlando, FL: Harcourt.

Winters, K. (2003). *Abe Lincoln: The boy who loved books*. (N. Carpenter, Illus.). New York: Simon & Schuster.

Chapter 7: March

Bagert, B. (2007). *Shout! Little poems that roar*. (S. Yoshikawa, Illus.). New York: Dial.

Bayer, J. (1984). *A my name is Alice*. New York: Dial Books.

Burg, B. (2002). *Outside the lines: Poetry at play*. (R. Gibbon, Illus.). New York: Putnam.

Dakos, K. (1995). *Mrs. Cole on an onion roll*. (J. Adinolfi, Illus.). New York: Simon & Schuster.

de Regniers, B. S., Moore, E., White, M. M., & Carr, J. (1988). *Sing a song of popcorn: Every child's book of poems*. (M. Brown et al., Illus.). New York: Scholastic.

Edwards, P. D. (1995). *Four famished foxes and Fosdyke*. New York: HarperCollins.

_____. (2001). *Slop goes the soup*. (H. Cole, Illus.). New York: Hyperion.

Florian, D. (1999). *Laugh-eteria*. San Diego: Harcourt.

_____. (2001). *Lizards, frogs, and polliwogs*. San Diego: Harcourt.

_____. (2003). *Bow wow meow meow: It's rhyming cats and dogs*. San Diego: Harcourt.

George, J. C. (2008). *The wolves are back*. (W. Minor, Illus.). New York: Dutton.

Gliori, D. (Ed.). (1997). *Poems go clang! A collection of noisy verse*. (D. Gliori, Illus.). Cambridge, MA: Candlewick.

Harley, A. (2006). *Sea stars: Saltwater poems*. (M. Butschler, Photographer). Honesdale, PA: Wordsong.

Hopkins, L. B. (1995). *Good rhymes, good times*. (F. Lessac, Illus.). New York: HarperCollins.

Hopkins, L. B. (Ed.). (1990). *Good books, good times*. (H. Stevenson, Illus.). New York: HarperCollins.

_____. (1996). *School supplies: A book of poems*. (R. Flower, Illus.). New York: Simon & Schuster.

_____. (2003). *A pet for me: Poems* (J. Manning, Illus.). New York: HarperCollins.

_____. (2004). *Wonderful words: Poems about reading, writing, speaking, and listening*. (K. Barbour, Illus.). New York: Simon & Schuster.

Lewis, J. P. (1996). *Riddle-icious*. (D. Tilley, Illus.). New York: Alfred A. Knopf.

Lillegard, D. (2001). *Hello school!* (D. Carter, Illus.). New York: Alfred A. Knopf.

MacDonald, R. (2003). *Achoo! Bang! Crash! The noisy alphabet*. Roaring Book Press.

Martin Jr., B., & Sampson, M. (2006). *I love our Earth*. (D. Lipow, Photographer). Watertown, MA: Charlesbridge.

Prelutsky, J. (1984). *The new kid on the block*. (J. Stevenson, Illus.). New York: Greenwillow.

_____. (1990). *Something big has been here*. (J. Stevenson, Illus.). New York: Greenwillow.

_____. (1996). *A pizza the size of the sun*. (J. Stevenson, Illus.). New York: Greenwillow.

_____. (2000). *It's raining pigs & noodles*. (J. Stevenson, Illus.). New York: Greenwillow.

_____. (2005). *Read a rhyme, write a rhyme*. (M. So, Illus.). New York: Knopf.

_____. (2008). *My dog may be a genius*. (J. Stevenson, Illus.). New York: Greenwillow.

_____. (2008). *Pizza, pigs, and poetry: How to write a poem*. New York: HarperCollins/Greenwillow.

Prelutsky, J. (Ed.). (1983). *The Random House book of poetry for children*. (A. Lobel, Illus.). New York: Random House.

_____. (1986). *Read-aloud rhymes for the very young*. (M. Brown, Illus.). New York: Knopf.

Reed, L., Wood, D., Burnett, S., & Noble, A. (1999). *Sing and read "red."* (A. Noble, Illus.). Crandall, TX: Frog Street Press.

Roemer, H. B. (2004). *Come to my party and other shape poems*. (H. Takahashi, Illus.). New York: Holt.

Rosenthal, M. (2007). *Phooey!* New York: HarperCollins/Joanna Cotler.

Schwartz, A. (1992). *Busy buzzing bumblebees and other tongue twisters*. (P. Meisel, Illus.). New York: HarperCollins.

Silverstein, S. (1974). *Where the sidewalk ends*. New York: HarperCollins.

_____. (1981). *A light in the attic*. New York: HarperCollins.

Yolen, J., & Peters, A. F. (Eds.). (2007). *Here's a little poem: A very first book of poetry*. Cambridge, MA: Candlewick.

Young, S. (1997). *The Scholastic rhyming dictionary*. New York: Scholastic.

Walker, A. (2006). *There is a flower at the tip of my nose smelling me.* (S. Vitale, Illus.). New York: HarperCollins.

Wolfe, F. (2001). *Where I live.* Toronto, Ontario: Tundra.

Chapter 8: April and May

Allen, J. (2000). *Are you a ladybug?* (T. Humphries, Illus.). New York: Kingfisher.

Arnosky, J. (2003). *All about sharks.* New York: Scholastic.

Aston, D. H. (2007). *A seed is sleepy.* (S. Long, Illus.). San Francisco, CA: Chronicle.

Bang, M. (2004). *My light.* New York: Scholastic.

Berkes, M. C. (2007). *Over in the jungle: A rainforest rhyme.* (J. Canyon, Illus.). Nevada City, CA: Dawn.

Christian, P. (2000). *If you find a rock.* (B. H. Lember, Photographer). San Diego: Harcourt.

Collard, S. B. (1997). *Animal dads.* (S. Jenkins, Illus.). New York: Houghton Mifflin.

_____. (1998). *Our wet world.* (J. M. Needham, Illus.). Watertown, MA: Charlesbridge.

Dahl, M. (2007). *If you were a synonym.* (S. Gray, Illus.). Minneapolis, MN: Picture Window.

Davies, N. (2001). *One tiny turtle.* (J. Chapman, Illus.). Cambridge, MA: Candlewick.

Doeden, M. (2008). *Thunderstorms.* Minneapolis, MN: Lerner.

Donohue, M. R. (2008). *Penny and the punctuation bee.* (J. Law, Illus.). Morton Grove, IL: A. Whitman.

Florian, D. (2000). *Mammalabilia.* Orlando, FL: Harcourt.

_____. (2007). *Comets, stars, the moon, and Mars.* Orlando, FL: Harcourt.

Gans, R. (1997). *Let's go rock collecting.* (H. Keller, Illus.). New York: HarperCollins.

Godkin, C. (2006). *Fire! The renewal of a forest.* Markham, Ontario: Fitzhenry and Whiteside.

Guiberson, B. Z. (2004). *Rain, rain, rain forest.* (S. Jenkins, Illus.). New York: Holt.

Hatkoff, I., Hatkoff, J., Hatkoff, C., & Uhlich, G. R. (2007). *Knut: How one little polar bear captivated the world.* (Zoo Berlin, Photographs). New York: Scholastic.

Hopkins, L. B. (Ed.). (1999). *Spectacular science: A book of poems.* (V. Halstead, Illus.). New York: Simon & Schuster.

Jenkins, S. (2006). *Almost gone: The world's rarest animals.* New York: HarperCollins.

Kompelien, T. (2007). *Cool rocks.* Edina, MN: ABDO.

Lewis, J. P. (2004). *Scien-trickery: Riddles in science.* (F. Remkiewicz, Illus.). Orlando, FL: Silver Whistle.

Locker, T. (1997). *Water dance.* New York: Harcourt.

Marzollo, J. (1996). *I am fire.* (J. Moffatt, Illus.). New York: Scholastic.

_____. (1996). *I am water.* (J. Moffatt, Illus.). New York: Scholastic.

_____. (1997). *I am an apple.* (J. Moffatt, Illus.). New York: Scholastic.

_____. (1997). *I'm a caterpillar.* (J. Moffatt, Illus.). New York: Scholastic.

_____. (1998). *I am a leaf.* (J. Moffatt, Illus.). New York: Scholastic.

_____. (1998). *I am a rock.* (J. Moffatt, Illus.). New York: Scholastic.

_____. (1998). *I am snow.* (J. Moffatt, Illus.). New York: Scholastic.

_____. (2000). *I am a star.* (J. Moffatt, Illus.). New York: Scholastic.

_____. (2000). *I am planet earth.* (J. Moffatt, Illus.). New York: Scholastic.

Mitchell, S. K. (2007). *The rainforest grew all around.* (C. McLennan, Illus.). Mount Pleasant, SC: Sylvan Dell.

Murphy, S. (2000). *Dave's down-to-earth rock shop.* (C. B. Smith, Illus.). New York: HarperCollins.

Paolilli, P., & Brewer, D. (2001). *Silver seeds: A book of nature poems.* New York: Puffin.

Patent, D. H. (1997). *Flashy fantastic rain forest frogs.* (K. J. Jubb, Illus.). New York: Walker.

Prager, E. J. (2001). *Volcano!* (N. Woodman, Illus.). Washington, D.C.: National Geographic Society.

Rockwell, A. (2001). *Bugs are insects.* (S. Jenkins, Illus.). New York: HarperCollins.

Schaefer, L. M. (2002). *What's up, what's down?* (B. Bash, Illus.). New York: HarperCollins.

Showers, P. (2001). *What happens to a hamburger?* (E. Miller, Illus.). New York: HarperCollins.

Sweeney, J. (1989). *Me and my place in space.* (A. Cable, Illus.). New York: Crown.

_____. (1999). *Me and my amazing body.* (A. Cable, Illus.). New York: Crown.

Walker, S. M. (2006). *Mystery fish: Secrets of the coelacanth.* (S. Gould, Illus.). Minneapolis, MN: Millbrook.

_____. (2008). *The search for Antarctic dinosaurs.* (J. Bindon, Illus.). Minneapolis, MN: Millbrook.

Wiesmuller, D. (2002). *In the blink of an eye.* New York: Walker.

Editing Checklist:

☐ I have spaces.
Finger
Space ↑ ↑

☐ WW
Word Wall
Words

☐ A̲
Beginning
Capital

☐ ⊙
Ending
Mark

Editing Checklist:

☐ I have spaces.
Finger
Space ↑ ↑

☐ WW
Word Wall
Words

☐ A̲
Beginning
Capital

☐ ⊙
Ending
Mark

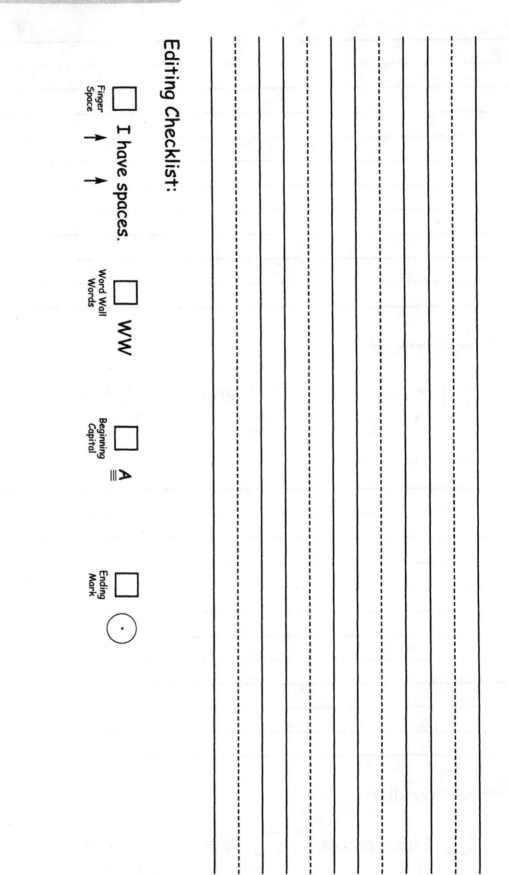

Editing Checklist:

☐ I have spaces.
Finger Space → →

☐ ww
Word Wall Words

☐ A̲̲
Beginning Capital

☐ ⊙
Ending Mark

Parent Note: Journals

Dear First-Grade Parents,

This is your child's first daily journal. Daily journal writing is an important component of our literacy program because it enables children to work at their instructional level. As students sound out words to write, they apply the phonics knowledge they acquire during our word study lessons. If students have a strong knowledge of phonics, daily writing fosters their ability to effectively communicate their ideas in a written format. Each day when children complete their journal they read it to an adult. At this time we encourage and support your child as he or she extends his or her writing skills. We focus on a wide range of skills, depending on the level of the child:

- Applying letter-sound knowledge to chop up and spell words
- Leaving spaces between words
- Printing legibly
- Writing a complete sentence
- Beginning each sentence with a capital letter and concluding each sentence with an ending mark
- Using the word wall and other print resources in our room to spell words correctly
- Utilizing word patterns to spell difficult words
- Adding details to words and illustrations

You can help your child with his or her journal writing by discussing different ideas to write about each day. Also, encourage your child to keep a journal at home for weekends, trips, and special events. Early pieces of writing such as these are wonderful keepsakes for the years to come! At the end of each month, I will send home your child's journal in the First-Grade Folder so that you can monitor the progress he or she is making in writing. **Please send your child's journal back to school after you have had time to enjoy it with your family.** I will save all of the students' journals until the end of the year, when we celebrate their accomplishments in writing by having a journal party. At that time I will send your child's journals home for you to keep. Thank you for your cooperation.

Enjoy!!

Your Child's Teacher

Parent Note: Parent Publishing Company

Dear _____,

Thank you for volunteering to type the pieces our students will write this year! We hope the following guidelines will help make your job easier and more enjoyable. We know you will love reading the children's fantastic ideas while you type!!

I. Editing

Before you get the piece, the students will have edited it and corrected beginning capitals, ending marks, and word wall words. We will "transcribe" (write underneath) to help you read their other words. We would greatly appreciate it if while you type you watch and correct these items:

- Spelling
- Punctuation
- Subject-verb agreement
- Tense agreement
- Any other grammatical errors that you see

We know this sounds like a big job, but once you start typing you will find it is natural for you to spell correctly and punctuate where needed.

II. Format

Enclosed are samples of finished pages—we will be using a half sheet format ($8\frac{1}{2} \times 5\frac{1}{2}$). You may send us full sheets and we will cut them to size.

III. Supplies

Please let us know when you run out of paper and we will supply more.

IV. Workload and Due Dates

The amount of stories will vary each quarter, but you should never have more than five or so during one week. We would appreciate having the typed stories back within two days, so students are able to illustrate them while the ideas are still fresh in their minds. We hope this letter helps get you started. If you find we did not answer a question or you need more information, please feel free to call, write, or e-mail. Thank you for helping to make our Writing Workshop an exciting and productive experience for our students.

Sincerely,

The First-Grade Team and Our Young Authors

Month-by-Month Trait-Based Writing Instruction © 2009 by Maria Walther and Katherine Phillips, Scholastic Professional.

Journal Writing Observations

Name _____

	September	October	November	December	January	February	March	April	May
Writes on a variety of topics									
Organizes ideas									
Chooses interesting words									
Varies sentence length									
Uses appropriate spacing between words									
Begins sentences with a capital letter									
Uses ending punctuation correctly									
Uses legible handwriting									
Attempts pre-phonetic spelling (LT, RS, SK) (light, rice, sink)									
Uses phonetic spelling (LIT, RIS, SIK)									
Uses transitional spelling (LITE, RICE, SINGK)									
Spells high-frequency words correctly									

Criteria

+   SECURE: Consistently demonstrates this writing skill/strategy

✓   DEVELOPING: Attempts this writing skill/strategy but is not yet consistent

–   BEGINNING: Little or no evidence or this writing skill/strategy

Month-by-Month Trait-Based Writing Instruction © 2009 by Maria Walther and Katherine Phillips, Scholastic Professional.

Editing Checklist:

☐ I have spaces.
Finger
Space

☐ WW
Word Wall
Words

☐ A
Beginning
Capital

☐ ⊙
Ending
Mark

My
Idea
Notebook

A Writing Center Publication

Name _____

My family . . . .

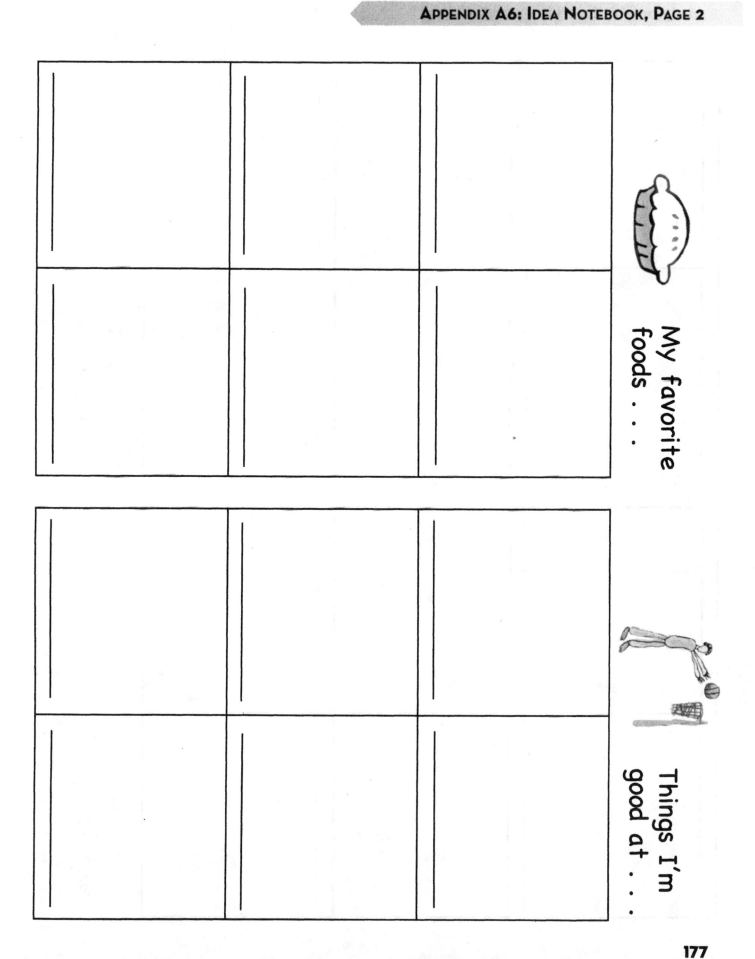

My favorite foods . . .

Things I'm good at . . .

My favorite animals . . .

Places I've been . . .

Name _____ Due Date: _____

Personal Narrative Planning Sheet

Dear Parents,

Next week during writing workshop your child will be writing a personal narrative about a special moment in his/her life. Please talk with your child about a special memory he or she has—it might be a birthday party, a recent vacation, a day at the pool, or another memorable event. **Affix a photograph of this special memory or have your child draw a picture of the event in the box below.**

Then, work with your child to write four words or phrases that describe the event. Here are a few examples to get you started!

A day at the pool: swim, read a book, play with friends, splash
A visit with Grandma: read, play, watch movies, bake cookies
The Cubs game: cheer, sing, eat hot dogs, they win!
Losing my tooth: wiggling, falls out, under pillow, tooth fairy

Event: _____

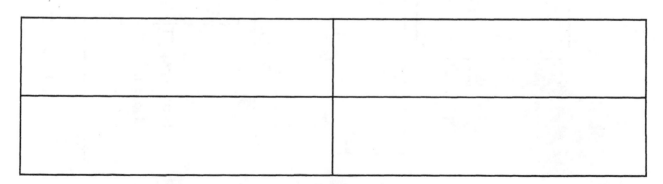

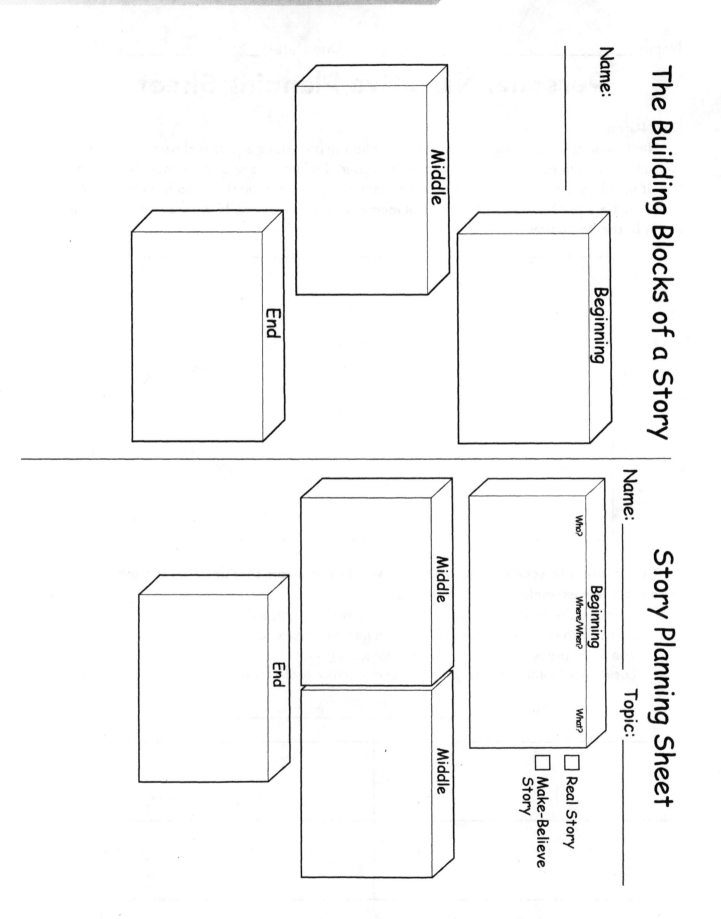

The Building Blocks of a Story

Name: _____

Middle

Beginning

End

Story Planning Sheet

Name: _____   Topic: _____

☐ Real Story

☐ Make-Believe Story

Beginning

Who?   Where/When?   What?

Middle

Middle

End

Name: _____

Story Planning Sheet

Topic: _____

☐ Real Story

☐ Make-Believe Story

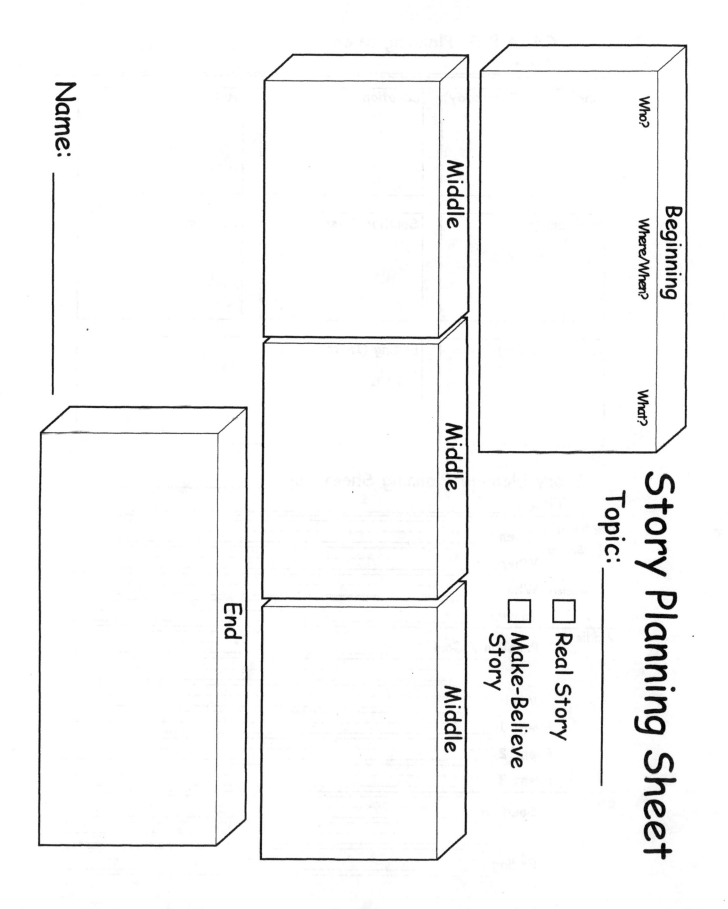

Beginning

Who? | Where/When? | What?

Middle

Middle

Middle

End

C.L.A.P.S. Planning Sheet   By:_____

Title :_____

Character (Somebody)	Location	Action (wanted)

Problem (but)	Solution 1 (so)	Solution 2 (so)

Solution 3 (so)	Ending (In the end)

Story Element Planning Sheet   By:_____

Title :_____

Beginning

Setting

When _____

Where _____

Characters **Who** _____

Romance _____

Middle

Problem / Goal _____

_____

Villain _____

Event 1 _____

Event 2 _____

Event 3 _____

End

Solution _____

_____

Ending _____

Month-by-Month Trait-Based Writing Instruction © 2009 by Maria Walther and Katherine Phillips, Scholastic Professional.

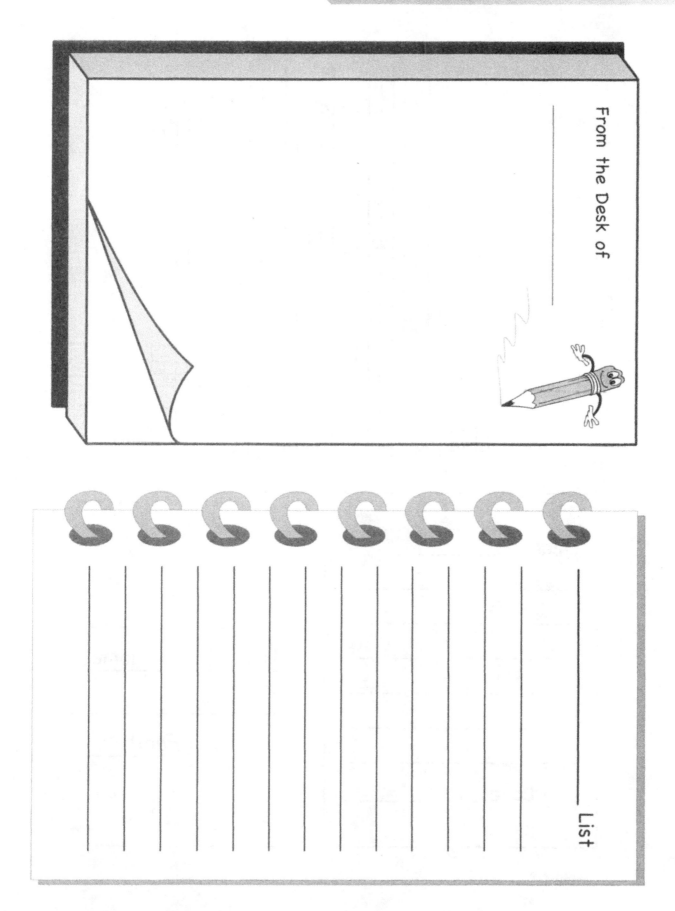

From the Desk of

List

Appendix A12: Postcard and Letter Writing Paper

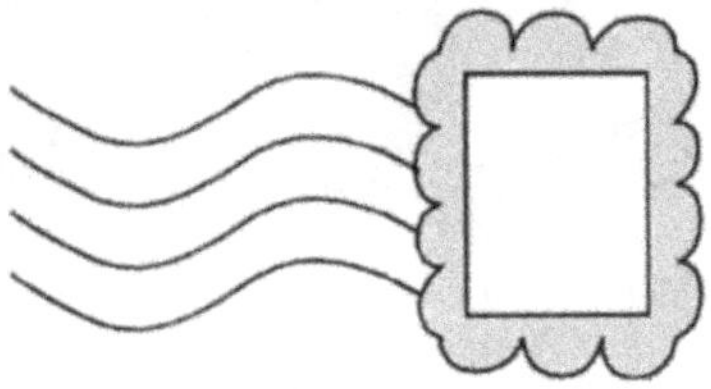

Dear __________,

____

____

____

____

____

____

Love, __________

____

Home Sweet Home

____

Planet Earth

My Interview Notebook

Interviewer: _____

My Biography Buddy is: _____

FAMILY

How many people are in your family? _____

How many brothers and sisters do you have? _____

What do you like to do together?
_____
_____

FRIENDS

What makes you a good friend?
_____
_____

What are your friends' names?
_____
_____

What do you like to do together?
_____
_____
_____

Month-by-Month Trait-Based Writing Instruction © 2009 by Maria Walther and Katherine Phillips, Scholastic Professional.

FAVORITES

What are your favorite foods?

_____

_____

_____

What are your favorite hobbies/activities?

_____

_____

_____

What are your favorite school subjects?

_____

_____

_____

FUN FACTS

What are your special talents?

_____

_____

What are some special places you've visited?

_____

_____

What is something funny that has happened to you?

_____

_____

Nonfiction Feature:

_____

Purpose:

_____

_____

Written and Illustrated by:

_____

TABLE OF CONTENTS

Month-by-Month Trait-Based Writing Instruction © 2009 by Maria Walther and Katherine Phillips, Scholastic Professional.

WHAT DOES A _____ LOOK LIKE?

Editing Checklist:

☐ I like books.
Finger
Space ↑ ↑

☐ WW
Word Wall
Words

☐ A
Beginning
Capital

☐ ⊙
Ending
Mark

A HOME FOR _____

Editing Checklist:

☐ I like books.
Finger
Space ↑ ↑

☐ WW
Word Wall
Words

☐ A
Beginning
Capital

☐ ⊙
Ending
Mark

FAVORITE FOODS

_____
- -
_____
- -
_____
- -
_____
- -
_____
- -

Editing Checklist:

☐ I like books. ☐ WW ☐ A ☐ ⊙
Finger Space ↑ ↑   Word Wall Words   Beginning Capital   Ending Mark

- -

FUN FACTS

_____
- -
_____
- -
_____
- -
_____
- -
_____
- -

Editing Checklist:

☐ I like books. ☐ WW ☐ A ☐ ⊙
Finger Space ↑ ↑   Word Wall Words   Beginning Capital   Ending Mark

CPSIA information can be obtained
at www.ICGtesting.com
Printed in the USA
LVHW021529180723
752677LV00009B/490

9 780545 066938